NATURAL DIGRESSIONS

A Natural History for the 21ˢᵗ Century

In Nature's infinite book of secrecy
A little I can read.

—William Shakespeare

Not Bad Monk.

Sturnus Publishing
33 W. Penny Road
South Barrington, IL 60010-9578

ISBN: 978-0-578-14417-790000

Printed in the United States on recycled paper.

Spreyer, Mark Frank, (1956-
Natural Digressions: A Natural History for the 21st Century

For Susan, for everything.

FOREWORD

As a naturalist and writer, I'm a firm believer in "reduce, reuse, and recycle." Natural Digressions' contents entered the literary recycling stream as stories in Stillman Nature Center's quarterly newsletter. In many cases, the essays have been reduced and reused in newspapers, magazines, and as hand-outs for college students. Some readers of those publications suggested that the articles should be recycled as a book. Here it is.

As you can see, most of the essays have been arranged taxonomically. Please go to a favorite subject and dig in. There is no reason to read Digressions in any particular order.

I thought it only appropriate that proceeds made from this book be given to Stillman Nature Center, my employer and a 501(c)(3) organization. I hope you enjoy what you find in the following pages. If not, rest assured that your money is going to help a worthwhile nature center.

—M. F. S.

TABLE OF CONTENTS

WILDFLOWERS

Bloodroot in bloom. Photo by Karen Lund.

I. WILDFLOWERS

Roses are red,
Violets are blue;
But they don't get around
Like the dandelions do.

—Slim Acres

CEREAL HERMAPHRODITES:
The Truth Behind Wildflower Names

The early blooming flowers that decorate the forest floor are some of the most welcome signs of spring. If you live anywhere from the Great Lakes south along the Appalachians or along the Mississippi or Ohio River Valleys, and have a chance to visit a wooded preserve in April or early May, you won't have to walk far from your car to find many of these delicate beauties.

After you learn to identify these plants, you can't help but wonder how they got names that are often as colorful as their blossoms. With that in mind, let's take a closer look at the names of four woodland wildflowers.

Virginia Bluebell or **Virginia Cowslip** *(Mertensia virginica)*
The nature center where I work is probably best known for its spectacular masses of Virginia Bluebells. Once you have seen its blue, bell-shaped flowers, the first name makes sense... but Cowslip? What kind of b—-s—- name is that? Actually, that's exactly what it is. Cowslip has its origin in the Anglo-Saxon word *cuslyppe, cu* meaning cow and *slyppe* for slop or dung.

Another wildflower, marsh marigold, also has cowslip as an alternate moniker. Marsh marigolds, as the name implies, prefers to grow in wet sites. Similarly, Virginia Cowslip favors moist shaded areas and bottomlands. It is likely that the ground in which these wildflowers grew reminded early European settlers of pastures laden with cow-slop. Or, perhaps, they were found blossoming in the *cuslyppe.*

Finally, the plant's genus or the first part of its scientific name, *Mertensia*, is for Franz Karl Mertens (1764-1831), a German botanist.

White or Large-flowered Trillium *(Trillium grandiflorum)*

With this trillium, if you know the common name, you are already familiar with the scientific name. This is, arguably, the most appropriately named of the forest wildflowers.

Everything about this plant comes in threes. It has three broad leaves, three white petals, three sepals, three-celled ovaries and its fruit, a red berry, features three ribs. It should come as no surprise that its genus name is derived from *tri*, Latin for three.

Although there are other trilliums that grow in the area, none will be confused with this largest and showiest representative of the clan. Its single white blossom, which inspired both common names, can grow to be four inches across. The Latin translation of large-flowered, *grandiflorum*, is this plant's species and the second part of its scientific name.

White Trout Lily alias Fawn Lily alias Dogtooth Violet alias Adder's-tongue *(Erythronium albidum)*

Unlike the other wildflowers, this one is named for its leaves, mottled leaves that are spotted like a trout or fawn. Plants with a single leaf will not flower while those with a pair of leaves can

4

be expected to flower. The pair of leaves also offers an additional explanation for the name fawn lily. As naturalist John Burroughs wrote at the turn of the twentieth century, "Its two leaves stand up like fawn's ears, and this feature, with its recurved petals, gives it an alert, wide-awake look."

The name dogtooth violet raises some problems. This plant is definitely a lily, not a violet. The flower is an inch wide with white petals that, as Burroughs describes, curve back.

The "dogtooth" does not refer to the flower but, rather, to the tooth-like shape of this plant's underground bulb. Why a dog's tooth? Why not a cat's tooth or a baby's tooth? Did someone just happen to have a dog's tooth laying around for comparison's sake? Perhaps, I'm barking up, I mean, under the wrong tree.

Then we get to adder's-tongue. Unless you have quite an imagination, there is nothing to suggest a snake's tongue on this wildflower. It is more likely that the plant reminded European settlers of some plant from the old country called adder's-tongue. All I can say is if this plant ever suffers a multiple personality disorder, it will have a ready name on hand for each of its personalities. (Speaking of personality disorders...well, we'll get to that later.)

Jack (or Jill) -in-the-pulpit *(Arisaema triphyllum)*

It is the peculiar design of its blossom that has earned this plant its common name. It sports a striped green hood or "pulpit" which curls over "Jack," a club-shaped organ known as a *spadix*. It is at the base of the spadix, where the tiny flowers, either male or female, are to be found. How can you tell a male Jack from a female Jill?

The simple answer is count the leaves. If it only has one three-parted leaf, it's a male. If it has two, it's a female. And yes, to you Latin scholars, the species name, *triphyllum*, refers to this wildflower's three-parted leaf.

The fascinating part of this species' natural history is that a particular plant's gender is negotiable. That is to say, one year's Jack may be next year's Jill. If a large female has a few bad years, researchers have found that in the following year it may produce only one leaf and flower as a male. The reverse is also true. Should that scrawny male enjoy good growing conditions, it can regain its status as a large, multi-leaved female.

This sequential hermaphroditism makes me wonder what we should properly call this wildflower. Jack-in-the-Pulpit? Jill-in-the-Pulpit? Wait a second, I've got it. The Cowslip reminds me of Chicago's championship basketball team, the Bulls. Of course, it's been a while since they won a championship. Be that as it may, the Bulls player I'm thinking of continues to make news. Why don't we call this gender-bending flower Dennis-in-the-pulpit?

SHRIEKING & BLOODY ROOTS

Contrary to the title, this will not be a botanical Halloween story. Instead, we are going to revisit the early blooming flowers that decorate the forest floor. In the previous essay, I wrote about four of these beauties: the Virginia bluebell, white trillium, trout lily, and jack-in-the-pulpit.

In this article, we'll briefly revisit the trout lily and introduce three more woodland wildflowers: wild geranium, mayapple, and bloodroot. Although Halloween comes in autumn, there are hints of haunting in the springtime woods.

Wild Geranium or Cranesbill *(Geranium maculatum)*

This wildflower, with deeply lobed leaves, typically grows in shady areas, reaches a height of one to two feet, and begins to blossom in the latter half of May. The blossoms have five petals, are pink to lavender in color, and are arranged in a loose cluster at the tip of the plant.

The flower becomes a pointed seed pod which resembles a crane's bill and explains the first part of its scientific name. *Geranium* comes from the Greek *geranos*, meaning crane. For the same reason, the genus name for the greenhouse geranium is *Pelargonium* which means storkbill.

As its seeds mature, cranesbill prepares to perform its own botanical sleight-of-hand. When fully ripened, the beaked pod splits into five segments that suddenly coil upward, scattering its seeds for a distance of several feet.

Mayapple or Mandrake *(Podophyllum peltatum)*
Resembling a cluster of stubby umbrellas,
colonies of mayapple can be found
growing in maple or oak woods as well
as on the edges of clearings. The leaves,
which are dark green above and light green
below, grow to a height of twelve to eighteen inches.
Like the trout lily, only double-leaved stems
produce flowers; single-leaved stems will not.

The flower is something to see, but you have to lift up the large
leaves to find it. As the name suggests, the flower appears in May
and it resembles an apple blossom. Mayapple's single, large (one to
two inch diameter), white, waxy flower is located at the fork of the
two leaves. The flower develops into an "apple" (a berry, actually)
that looks like a small lemon. Although the yellow pulp in this fruit
is edible, the seeds it contains are poisonous.

The name mandrake comes from an unrelated southern European
plant that has a similar looking root. The root of the Old World
mandrake was once thought to resemble human form and to shriek
when plucked.

Bloodroot *(Sanguinaria canadensis)*
This native poppy's common name comes from its red sap. Similarly,
its genus same, like the word sanguine, refers to the blood-red color
of the plant's juice. American Indians used this plant's sap to dye
baskets, fabric, and for painting skin. It was also used as an insect

repellent. Early wildflower books will list this plant as red puccoon. Puccoon comes from an Algonquin term for a plant with red juice.

Bloodroot's gorgeous flower is one-and-a-half inches across and has from eight to fifteen petals. Four of the petals are usually just a bit larger than the rest. Unfortunately, the fragile blossom is only visible, here in northern Illinois, for a day or two in April.

At first, as illustrated by the color plate on page 1, the plant's distinctively-lobed leaf is found under the flower, clasping the stem. Later, the leaves will be larger than the flower, growing to be six inches wide and nearly a foot tall. Bloodroot's variable leaf can have five to nine blunt-toothed lobes.

Bloodroot typically grows in small clumps or drifts. All the flowers in a drift can trace their roots, so to speak, back to an individual "parent" plant. Not surprisingly, the leaf shape in each clump will be consistent. If the parent plant had seven lobes, then all the bloodroot leaves in that drift will have seven lobes.

Bloodroot prefers growing in moist and shady conditions. The floor of a mature maple forest, for instance, is a good place to look for drifts of bloodroot. Bloodroots effectiveness as a bug repellent is debatable since ants collect and help disperse bloodroot seeds through the woods.

Now You See 'em, Now You Don't

Another seemingly magical occurrence, a wildflower disappearing act, occurs each spring in the woods. Some of the early blooming flowers found on the forest floor will sprout, mature, flower and produce seeds between the time the snow melts and the tree canopy fully develops. In the summer, there is no leaf, no flower, no sign that these plants ever existed. The energy the wildflowers have gathered from the spring sun will be stored in their roots and used next year to repeat their life cycle.

Don't be fooled by this disappearing act; these are not short-lived plants. For example, studies conducted in southern Wisconsin indicated that the average age of a trout lily colony is 145 years. Some colonies were found to be over 300 years old! Short lived? Not hardly.

You, on the other hand, have only a brief time to enjoy these flowers. So, when you have a little free time visit a nearby forest. One last thought about a woodland wildflower walk. While I can guarantee that you won't be sharing the trail with any shrieking human-like roots, I must warn you that, according to Alice Morse Earle in her 1901 volume *Old Time Gardens*, some flowers are inherently mysterious. She writes:

> *In childhood I absolutely abhorred bloodroot; it seemed to me a fearsome thing...I remember well my dismay, it was so pure, so sleek, so innocent of face, yet bleeding at a touch like a murdered man...*

THE DEVIL & ST. ANNE

My father, bless his heart, chose to let a wild meadow grow in our sizable backyard. It was just mowed once a year in the fall. So in the summer, I had the opportunity to wander through the field and chew on a sweet timothy stem or watch the assortment of insects attracted to milkweeds.

One of the best meadow color combinations was the blue of chicory combined with the white of Queen Anne's lace. So let's investigate Queen Anne's lace *(Daucas carota)*. We'll save chicory for another day.

A quick look at the illustration (p. 15) and I'm sure you'll recognize this lacy flat-topped flower, also known as wild carrot. It can be found growing from the Atlantic to the Pacific in old fields, pastures, and along roadsides.

The "blossoms" are composed of hundreds of tiny five-petal florets, called an umbel, which can be up to five inches across. Most of them are all white. Some, though, have a single burgundy floret in the center of the white multitude.

Which Queen Anne?

As the story goes, Queen Anne was busy stitching lace when she pricked her finger and a single drop of blood landed in the center of the white flower cluster. The question is, which Queen Anne?

If we agree that the plant name originated in England, the general consensus is Queen Anne of Great Britain and Ireland who was reported to be plain but with a "harmonious voice."

Others have suggested it could have been Anne Boleyn, Anne of Cleves, or even Anne of Denmark, the wife of James I of England, who used to decorate her hair with wild carrot.

If not an English Anne, things get even more interesting. My favorite is the religious conspiracy theory. Jesus' grandmother, St. Anne, was the patron saint of lacemakers and sometimes called the "queen of heaven."

During the Reformation, Martin Luther was especially unhappy with Anne's veneration. So, according to this theory, the Protestants came up with a non-Catholic version of how the wild carrot came by its royal heritage.

Blood Sample

Let's get back to the red floret, does it have a purpose? Charles Darwin weighed in with the following comment, "...it cannot be supposed that this one flower makes the large white umbel at all more conspicuous to insects."

Fair enough, what then can we suppose of this one red floret? Research suggests that those blossoms with the tiny purple accessory enjoy a greater degree of pollination success. Why?

It is thought that predatory insects, such as ambush and assassin bugs, mistake the dark floret for an ant or juicy aphid. So they stalk their prey across the white umbel, pollinating the florets with each stealthy step.

Colonist or "Invader?"

Different reasons have been offered for why the Virginia colonists brought Queen Anne's lace to the new country. Some say for food, others say as a medicinal herb, while still others claim it was used to decorate the settlers' flowerbeds, sort of a botanical reminder of home.

Perhaps the correct answer is all of the above. You'd have to be pretty hungry, though, to find the fibrous, white root of wild carrot to be anything other than a food of last resort.

The term colonist applies not only to the folks who delivered Queen Anne's lace to North America but to the plant itself. As one British biologist explains, colonists "are species whose ecological style is to keep moving to fresh territory...." Weeds, he continues, "are simply organisms somebody would like removed."

And boy, did some farmers want to be rid of Queen Anne's lace. After cows ate it, their milk took on a bitter taste. Wild carrot, they learned, is one tough plant surviving repeated grazings, mowings, and various attempts at removing.

Queen Anne's lace was so disliked that some farmers dubbed it "devil's plague," quite a fall for a plant possibly named after Saint Anne.

Nowadays, disliked plant colonists are called "invaders" by some environmental zealots. When you see this word being used to describe naturalized plants and animals, be on the alert.

As ecologist Mark Davis wrote in 2009:

> *I have never liked the term 'invasion'... along with its accompanying military metaphors. Although the usage of military language may help to attract a group of highly motivated supporters, this same language may help foment a strongly confrontational approach...*

To build on Davis' point, picture a Canada goose protecting its nest. It is one thing to observe that a goose is aggressively defending its eggs, a natural behavior, and entirely another thing to label the goose as an aggressor.

A weed taking root in a new territory illustrates a natural adaptation. Calling this sprout an "invader" suggests a hostile intent. Plants are, of course, incapable of hostility.

Bringing our discussion back to wild carrot, it is a plant colonist transported to North America by human colonists. It did not invade, it was invited.

For You Plant Inviters

The simplest way to grow Queen Anne's lace is to gather the seeds in late summer and plant them in autumn.

You could also transplant them. If you choose this method, dig the young, first-year plants and make sure to get the entire root.

One of the benefits of having wild carrot in your garden is that its leaves are a favorite food for black swallowtail *(Papilio polyxenes)* caterpillars. These native butterflies would add a beautiful accent to anyone's yard.

Since Queen Anne's lace is a biennial, you should transplant or sow seeds for two years in a row. Then, you can look forward to seeing this delicate flower, supported by a tough plant, each and every summer.

Back Across the Pond

If you'd rather curse naturalized plants than grow them, I'll leave you with one last thought. The following was written nearly a hundred years ago by W. Barbellion, a short-lived but insightful British naturalist:

> *In the enfranchised mind of the scientific naturalist, the usual feelings of repugnance simply do not exist. Curiosity conquers prejudice.*

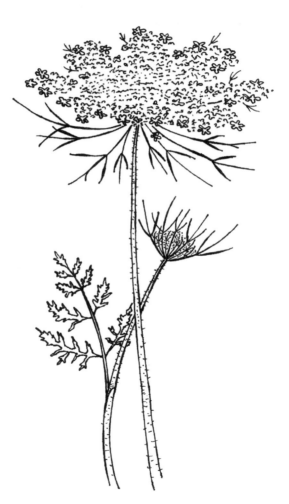

SILPHIUMS OF SUMMER

While teaching at a local community college, I was asked to introduce classes to prairies in late winter. Trying to sell this habitat while standing in clumps of cold, wet, brown (if the snow has melted) grasses and decaying vegetation can be something of a challenge.

One genus, though, is there to lend this desperate instructor a hand, the *Silphiums*. This group includes prairie dock *(Silphium terebinthinaceum)*, compass plant *(S. laciniatum)* and cup-plant *(S. perfoliatum)*. Let's take a closer look at these year-round stand-outs.

All Hands on Dock

Prairie Dock grows in clumps that, in the winter landscape, can be spotted several hundred feet away. Why so visible? Because their leaves are huge, measuring sixteen inches high and twelve inches across.

The prominent leaves also offer students an interesting tactile experience. They are sandpaper rough, particularly on the back surface. This coating of prickly hairs traps a thin layer of still air immediately adjacent to the leaf's surface. When you grow out on the hot, open prairie, moisture conservation is job one. The unshaven leaf's calm layer of air reduces the drying effect of harsh winds. This scratchy surface does not, however, make it less tasty.

Whether it is the bison of the past or the cattle of today, young prairie dock leaves are on the menu for large herbivores. If an area is overgrazed, the docks will quickly decrease.

John Curtis describes a virgin prairie in Wisconsin that, in 1940, was purchased and used as a pasture by the new owner. He writes that the horses and cattle sought out prairie docks and compass plants "like hidden candy at a child's birthday party."

Silphium Similarities

The candy simile is an appropriate one. Several members of this genus produce a chewable sap or rosin that was favored by both Native Americans and early settlers. Is it any wonder how rosinweed *(Silphium integrifolium)* got its common name?

While we're at it, all the *Silphiums* have very similar flowers, bright yellow in color and two to four inches across. All of the ones mentioned here bloom between July and September.

As with the closely related sunflowers, what appears to be a large single flower is actually a "composite" of many tiny flowers. What looks like petals are ray flowers while the center is composed of a dense cluster of disk flowers.

Interestingly, with sunflowers it is the disk flowers that become seeds. With silphiums, it is the ray flowers that produce seeds.

Like sunflowers, silphiums are tall. For example, prairie dock flowers can reach a height of nine feet and compass plant flowers can top ten feet.

Pointing the Way

Much as *Silphium* flowers are similar, the leaves are not. While dock leaves are as broad as a shovel blade, the compass plant leaves are dissected like a two-sided rake.

The coarsely-textured leaves, which are clumped at the plant's base, are one to three feet tall and up to two feet wide.

As some of you may know, the leaf arrangement is what earned this *Silphium* its common name. Compass plant leaves generally align themselves in a north-south direction, a trait pioneers found quite useful. By minimizing the surface area facing south, the plant keeps water loss to a minimum.

In decades past, compass plants were accurate indicators of original prairie soils. Today, things are a bit different. Since it can be easily propagated from seed, compass plants are now often found growing where a human chose to plant them.

Off With Their Heads!

If you are human who is growing some *Silphiums*, keep an eye out for the head-clipping weevil *(Haplorhynchites aeneus)*.

According to University of Illinois researchers, this weevil causes significant damage to *Silphiums* by clipping flowering stems and severing resin canals. Not surprisingly, the weevils inflict more damage where the diversity of *Silphium* species is low. It's enough to drive you to drink which brings us to...

Cup-plant

As with compass plant, the leaves are this *Silphium's* most distinctive feature. Unlike dock or compass plant, cup-plant's leaves are arranged in pairs clasping the plant's stout, square stem.

The basically triangular leaves are six to twelve inches long and four to eight inches wide. Where they join together, they curve downward and form a deep cup. This formation not only gave this plant its common name but also its species moniker, *perfoliatum* or perforated leaf.

The leaves do, indeed, collect water that is enjoyed by many small animals. I once saw a goldfinch stop for a drink while looking for seeds in the former flowerheads. Tree frogs can also be found in this plant's small, elevated pools.

If you'd like to attract some of these interesting critters to your yard, cup-plants might be for you. They'll do well in sun or partial shade but will need some room. Cup-plants self-sow readily and can grow to a height of eight feet.

One More Thing

Don't confuse prairie dock with the non-native common burdock. While both have large leaves, burdock has pink blossoms which turn into those sticky burs which most dog owners are, unfortunately, quite familiar with.

Of course, you might find a burdock growing near a prairie dock. If so, you know what you'll have? A pair-a-docks.

NATURE'S NUTS... AND SEEDS AND FRUITS

The trees in apple orchards
With fruit are bending down...
September days are here,
With summer's best of weather
And autumn's best of cheer.

—Helen Hunt Jackson

What fall festival isn't complete without apple cider? Who hasn't watched a squirrel collecting acorns? O.K., maybe it was sneaking some sunflower seeds from your bird feeder but you know what I mean. It's harvest time on the calendar. We humans tend to think of tasty meals at this time of year. Nature is planning for or, should I say, planting the next generation. Let's take a closer look at the different ways nature does this. It isn't all about food.

A Seedy Business

Seeds are the point in being a plant. If you are an annual or biennial, your genes will be gone in a year or two if your seeds don't succeed. Even perennials aren't going to be green forever.

Just producing viable seeds, however, does not guarantee a plant's future. If seeds only fell under the parent plant, the young seedlings would all have to compete with the larger established plant for water, nutrients, soil, and sunlight.

No, that's not a good plan. The seeds need to be dispersed to new sites that, hopefully, will provide hospitable surroundings where the seedlings can take root. Nature has come up with a variety of strategies to do just that.

Floaters

Of course, not all seeds are produced in autumn. Anyone who has cleaned cottonwood seeds from their screens or swept maple "helicopters" off their driveway knows that seeds fall for months.

I like to refer to these seeds, along with the milkweed "parachutes" that are seen in the fall, as "floaters." That is, they are designed to float or glide in the air and be dispersed by the wind. A partial list of other airborne floaters includes dandelion, goat's beard, thistle, dogbane, elm, and ash.

While many seeds can be transported by moving water, some are designed for that purpose. Water lilies and coconuts immediately come to mind. Less showy examples would include certain sedges which have seeds that contain pockets of air. These sedge seeds can float on water for several months before finding conditions suitable for germination.

Shooters

Some plants aren't counting on a well-timed gust of wind or water current to disperse their fruit. Instead, they fire their seeds into the great green yonder. In particular, I'm thinking of wild geranium and jewelweed.

Wild geranium, often called cranesbill, is a woodland wildflower that sports a pointed seed pod that resembles a crane's bill. When fully ripened, the beaked pod splits into five segments that suddenly coil upward, scattering its seeds for a distance of several feet.

Jewelweed is also known as touch-me-not for a good reason. A member of the *Impatiens* genus, the flower develops into an elastic five-chambered capsule. Touching the ripe fruit causes the capsule to open explosively, expelling its tiny seeds to a distance of as much as four feet. If you've never touched a loaded jewelweed five-shooter, as Richard Headstrom writes, "I guarantee you will jump at the unexpected volley from the miniature machine gun."

Hitchhikers

Anyone who has brushed these out of their pet's fur or picked them off their socks knows about hitchhikers. Seeds which hitch rides by hooking themselves to fur or fabric include burdock, cocklebur, sticktight, tick-trefoil, and sweet cicely, just to name a few.

I mention the first two since they are said to have inspired the invention of an everyday material. In 1948, George de Mestral, an amateur Swiss naturalist, took his dog for a walk. Once home, he had to remove many burs from the dog's fur and his own pants.

Being curious, he turned his microscope on the seed heads and noticed how the numerous small hooks on the seeds had attached themselves to loops in the fabric of his pants. Mestral had an idea for a new fastener.

By 1955, the inventor had patented his design for a "hook and loop fastener." Mestral went on to form Velcro Industries.

Lunchables

If you can't hitch a ride on the outside of an animal, why not ride on the inside? This brings us to wildlife food or, what I like to call, lunchables. The list of edible wild fruits is indeed a long one. A sampling would include plums, raspberries, crabapples, grapes, mulberries, acorns, hazelnuts, elderberries, and cherries.

For example, let's take a closer look at cherries. Approximately 100 species of wildlife dine on juicy wild cherries. Actually, the wildlife is enjoying flavorful seed containers. As you probably know, the cherry pit or seed is relatively smooth and hard. Not surprisingly, it passes through an animal's digestive tract unharmed, only to be deposited in a convenient pile of manure quite some distance from where it was first ingested.

Drinkables

While these various approaches to plant distribution do work, humans can be a little more single-minded when it comes to furthering plant distribution. This brings me back to apple cider. In order to make cider, you squeeze the juice from apples in cider presses. The leftover pressings contain, as you might imagine, an abundance of apple seeds.

One dedicated apple lover, Jonathan Chapman aka Johnny Appleseed, repeatedly visited the cider presses of western

Pennsylvania to gather apple seeds with which to plant new trees. Domestic apple trees, by the way, only existed on the East Coast since it was early colonists who first brought them to this continent.

By the time of his death in 1847, the seeds from those presses grew into apple orchards scattered across thousands of square miles of what is now Indiana and Ohio.

If you prefer a more potent drinkable derived from a flavorful seed container, I'll leave you with another verse from Helen Hunt Jackson.

> *Then for "October Month" they put a rude illuminated cut—*
> *Reaching ripe grapes from off the vine, or pressing them or tunning*
> *wine; or something to denote that there was vintage at this time of year.*

INSECTS

A long-horned grasshopper. Photo by Marek.

II. INSECTS

*...it is impossible carefully to watch the proceedings of
any insect, however insignificant, without feeling that no writer
of fiction ever invented a drama of such absorbing interest as is
acted daily before our eyes, though to indifferent spectators.*

—J. G. Wood

Author's Note: *This essay was written during an emergence of periodical cicadas in the Chicago area.*

THE SUMMER OF CICADAS

By the time you see this, you probably will have read more than one account of this insect's basic life history. So, let me see if I can find something a bit different about cicadas to share with you.

Ever since the Pilgrims misidentified them, many have confused cicadas with locusts. Locusts are a variety of short-horned grasshopper that come equipped with large back legs for jumping. Among many differences, cicadas are not leapers and do not have over-sized rear legs.

A modern musical icon, Bob Dylan, is one of those to have made this entomological error. His song "Day of the Locusts" (©1970 Big Sky Music) was inspired, in a troubling way, by cicadas.

Took hold of my sweetheart and away we did drive,
Straight for the hills, the black hills of Dakota,
Sure was glad to get out of there alive.
And the locusts sang, well, it give me a chill,

Hey Mr. Tambourine Bug

To further the confusion, both cicadas and locusts make sounds in the summer but they play different percussive instruments. The grasshopper rubs a scraper on its wings against a series of projections on those large hind legs. It reminds me of that ribbed wooden block I used to rub with a stick in elementary school. In the locust's case, the result is a pitch-less mechanical sound.

Before we explain the cicada's instrument, a brief review of anatomy is needed. Insects have three body parts: head, thorax, and abdomen. The thorax is the center section where the legs and wings are attached. It is also where the cicada's tambourine, so to speak, can be found.

To be precise, it is on the last segment of the thorax that the cicada has two hollow cavities that are covered on one side with a membrane similar to a drum head. These drum heads are not struck with a leg or wing; they are vibrated by muscles which are attached to them.

Now a chubby little cicada has a large, mostly empty abdomen. The vibrations from the nearby thorax are amplified in this hollow chamber. The resulting cacophony attracts other cicadas and creeped Dylan out.

When the cicadas sing, a colleague refers to them as the "summer bugs." Yes, cicadas are here every summer. There are over 75 species of cicada in the eastern half of the country and most of them have a much shorter life cycle then the periodical cicada. Thanks to their summer performances, one group of short-lived cicadas are known as the dog-day cicadas. Each species has its own distinct call that I'm sure helps out when you are looking for an appropriate mate.

Timing is Everything

Speaking of other species, the periodical cicada from the South emerges every thirteen years. It doesn't take a rocket scientist to recognize that 13 and 17 are prime numbers. You might recall that a prime number can only be divided by itself or one without the answer having a fraction.

One explanation for the extreme periodical nature of the insect's emergence goes as follows. By flooding the market with cicadian appetizers, the supply of insects overwhelms all possible demands made by predators. This explanation is called predator satiation.

But couldn't this strategy be adapted over a fewer number of years? Why set the record for longest insect life cycle? Evolutionary biologist Stephen Jay Gould had some interesting observations on this hypothesis.

Gould wrote that many potential predators have 2-5 year life cycles which, not surprisingly, coincide with the life-cycles of the of the dog-day or annual cicadas. These "annual" cicadas, by the way, generally emerge later in the summer than their periodical counterparts.

Now, let's say that the periodical cicada came out every ten years. Given that 10 is divisible by both 2 and 5, these cicadas are going to be on somebody's menu but 13 and 17 don't line up with any predator's life cycle.

Some moths have been able to reduce predation by jamming a bat's radar. The possum does the same by playing dead when it isn't. The periodical cicada adjusts its calendar.

As Gould concluded, "It is sometimes advantageous to put all your eggs in one basket— but be sure to make enough of them, and don't do it too often." (See *Cicada Basics* on following page.)

Giant Cicada Killers

One can imagine all manner of birds and mammals dining on cicadas but I want to draw your attention to a cicada predator I first saw decades ago.

I was about to band a bird in rural Kansas when the biggest damn wasp I had ever seen loudly buzzed by. I was so startled that the bird escaped my grip. Insect net in hand, I went after this monster. He seemed to be carrying something. Unfortunately, he zipped through and around some trees and disappeared.

Later, I saw one in an insect collection at the Audubon Camp in Wisconsin. It had the perfect name, giant cicada killer. The female, the larger of the genders and the one with a stinger, can be about two inches long. I definitely had seen a female in action.

Cicada killers are solitary wasps (also called sand hornets) that burrow six to ten inches in loose or sandy soils. Golfers take note, these hornets are fond of sand traps.

At the end of the burrow are three to four cells where one to two cicadas are placed. The cicada killer lays one egg in each cell.

The wasp's name isn't exactly accurate. Her sting actually paralyzes rather than kills the cicada. That way, when junior hatches, it will be able to feed on the still living or, should I say, the living, still-cicada. Think of it as the insect equivalent of "night of the living dead." With this fate in mind, being gobbled by a crow or a possum doesn't seem so bad!

Looking Back

By now, you'll have stories to tell about this year's emergence. Back in 1990, people in Chicago were using snow shovels to clear sidewalks of dead cicadas. In 1956, 311 emergence holes per square yard were counted in some forested areas near Chicago. Hmmm, 1956 was the year I first emerged. [Insert your own joke here.]

On that personal note, I'll leave you with a few more Dylan lyrics.

And the locusts sang, yeah, it give me a chill,
Oh, the locusts sang such a sweet melody.
Oh, the locusts sang their high whining trill,
Yeah, the locusts sang and they were singing for me.

PERIODICAL CICADA BASICS

Description: These robust insects are around 1.25 inches long with a three inch wingspan. The wings are clear with an orange sheen and reddish-orange trim along the leading wing margins. The underside of the abdomen is reddish-brown to yellow. Their bulging eyes are dark red.

Emerging: Cicada nymphs, or immatures, feed on sap sucked from the roots of woody plants for 17 years. They dig exit tunnels, 18 to 24 inches long, to the surface. The exit holes are a half-inch across.

Maturing: Like the annual cicadas do each year, the immature periodical cicadas crawl up on tree trunks, shrubs, or your deck. They split their skin and the adults crawl out leaving a translucent shell of skin behind.

Breeding: For roughly two weeks, male cicadas call to attract females. As their singing diminishes, the adult males' brief lives are ending.

Laying Eggs: After mating, females deposit 400 to 600 eggs in slits in branches. Eggs are laid in more than 70 species of trees including oak, hickory, apple, elm, ash, walnut and redbud. Six to eight weeks later, the nymphs hatch, drop to the ground, and begin their lengthy subterranean life.

Backyard Notes: As noted above, females lay eggs in tree branches. Unless it is a young, transplanted tree like those found in nurseries or orchards, serious damage is not a concern. Wrapping vulnerable branches with cheesecloth will protect them. While I'm at it, cicadas don't spread disease or pose a threat to humans. Also, if Fido partakes in some entomophagy, there's no need to worry.

DRAGONS AND DAMSELS

Warm weather brings out the bloodsuckers. In spring, the ticks start us off, followed by the mosquitoes and soon, the biting flies. Some recommend bat or purple martin houses to solve this problem. You see, these houses are supposed to attract residents that will eat copious amounts of flying, blood-sucking insects. Some lucky folks do, indeed, attract the desired bats or birds. Many other people, who dutifully build and put up these houses, wait year after year after year after year after year. No bats, no martins - many, many hungry mosquitoes.

Underwater Nymphs

If you live by a pond or lake, you probably know that's where the mosquitoes lay their eggs. It is in the water that they live the first part of their lives. So what should you do, drain the pond? No, of course not. In and over your pond live the mosquito hawks, better known as dragonflies, that fly faster than most insects and come equipped with giant traps for mouths. If they don't get the mosquitoes, their sidekicks, the damselflies, will.

Both dragonflies and damselflies belong to the insect Order Odonata which refers to their mandibles or mouthparts. Like mosquitoes, dragonfly larvae, also called nymphs, live in the water. Their lower lip (labium) is long, about a third of their body length, and hinged. In a blink of an eye the lip is thrust forward and prey is grabbed by two claw-like lobes called palps. One of the favorite things grabbed by hungry dragonfly larvae is mosquito larvae.

If you're living in the water, like dragonfly and damselfly larvae, you need some way to get oxygen. Similar to fish, these insects use gill-like structures. These gills can be an easy way to separate the two groups. The slender damselfly larva has three leaf-like gills that look like a multi-pronged tail. The larger and stockier dragonfly nymph has rectal gills which, hidden inside the tip of its abdomen, are not visible.

When the larvae are done growing, they crawl out of the water and rest on a nearby plant stem, stick or dock timber. The nymphal skin is cracked open and a newly minted adult dragonfly or damselfly emerges. It is always a special treat, here at the nature center, when visiting students can watch an adult dragonfly beat its wings for the first time.

Right Wingers & Straight Wingers

On a hot summer day, watching the dragons and damsels can prove to be quite entertaining. The adult dragonflies, particularly the larger ones, will roam some distances in search of prey. If you're by the pond's edge for a while, you'll notice that the mosquito hawks keep to the higher regions, above the water, coursing back and forth, passing the same point at intervals of a few minutes. Odds are these are males patrolling their territory. Other males of the same species will be chased off, while females, as you might expect, are usually courted.

As you watch, you'll probably notice that dragonflies, which can fly up to 35 miles per hour, hold their wings in a distinctive manner. How they hold their wings is another way to separate the closely related dragonflies and damselflies. When at rest, a dragonfly holds its wings out, at right angles to its body. The damselfly holds its wings lengthwise, directly over its thin body. In flight, the slower damselflies flutter while dragonflies zip and dart over the pond.

Some of the most common dragonflies you'll see skimming over a lake's surface belong to the family of dragonflies known as — ready for this — the common skimmers. Most dragonflies with colored spots or bands on their wings will belong to this family. With many of the member species, their bodies are shorter than their wingspans.

Compared to an ant or ladybug, dragonflies are big but not nearly as big as they were in their heyday, during the Permian period about 250 millions years ago. Fossils indicate that some species had wingspans exceeding two feet, nearly four times bigger than today's largest dragonfly. I'd hate to see the mosquitoes they were hunting!

Wizards of the Air

So you have to wonder, how did those fossil dragonflies get so big? Although superficially resembling them, these giants weren't true dragonflies; they were griffenflies, evolutionary precursors to today's dragonflies. In order to answer the size question, a quick review of insect respiration is needed.

Insects lack lungs or a nose or other mammal breathing apparatus. Instead, air enters their bodies through spiracles, tiny valve-like openings along the sides of their bodies. From there, the air diffuses through their bodies through a series of tubes known as tracheae. The tracheae are largest at the spiracles and then branch into smaller tubes as they reach into the insect's tissues.

As air follows these tubes through the insect's body, more and more oxygen is absorbed by the dragonfly's tissues. There is a limit to how far diffusion can move air and still be providing an adequate supply of oxygen. Keep in mind that today's air is a little less than 21% oxygen.

Imagine if the air had a higher level of oxygen, say 30%. With this increased supply, air could continue to provide oxygen as it traveled through the more extensive respiratory system that larger invertebrates would require. Indeed, fossil studies indicate that the atmosphere during the time of griffenflies was, most likely, richer in oxygen. This theory might also explain why the griffenflies kept company with giant millipedes and scorpions.

Mosquito Hawks

But enough of insect anatomy, let's get back to those "giant dragonflies." Not surprisingly, many a bird watcher has trained his or her binoculars on dragonflies buzzing along a shoreline. After all, dragonflies are out during the day, they're colorful, and they are active in mid-summer when the bird life gets to be a bit dull. But instead of being a bird or dragonfly watcher, picture yourself as a griffenfly watcher. This is exactly what David Grimaldi and Michael S. Engel do in their book *Evolution of Insects*. They write:

> ...*imagine how these insects flew, perhaps streaking through Paleozoic swamps and forests, landing on unsuspecting animals like a bird of prey. At their prodigious size, they must have preyed on virtually all other insects and even small vertebrates.*

Now that's what I call a mosquito hawk!

MIMICRY: A SPITTIN' IMAGE

Normally, when you see a story about nature's mimics you'll read about how the viceroy butterfly has evolved to look like the monarch or how some bug looks like a stick or leaf. Then you're shown a picture and you say, "Isn't that amazing." Well, when I'm done, you're going to say, "Isn't that disgusting!"

Faux Feces

Take that viceroy, for example. Everyone tells you how this pretty orange-and-black butterfly looks like the pretty orange-and-black monarch, but they don't tell you that the viceroy caterpillar doesn't look anything like a monarch caterpillar. In fact, it looks like crap, bird crap to be precise.

Think about it. You're a hungry bird or toad looking for a juicy caterpillar. You're scanning the bushes and leaves and what do you see plopped on a leaf, a juicy bird dropping. So, you move on not noticing that the bird dropping might just be crawling over to nibble on the edge of the leaf. Talk about effective mimicry!

This strategy is so effective that other butterflies and moths have caterpillars that look like gross guano. Interestingly, the viceroy caterpillar doesn't stop mimicking when it stops growing. Once reaching full size, as you may know, a caterpillar transforms into a chrysalis before it emerges as a butterfly. The monarch's chrysalis is jade green with spots of gold. Guess what the viceroy's looks like. You got it, a glob of bird poop hanging from the bottom of a leaf.

A Spittin' Image

If you take a walk around our nature center in late spring, you'll notice other globs sticking to leaves. These look all the world like spit. It is as if someone in desperate need of a spittoon went for a walk slinging saliva every which way.

Is some bug mimicking spit? No. Even though it's been called cuckoo spit or frog spit, wild animals are not in the habit of drooling, willy-nilly, across the landscape. If they were, perhaps an insect would have something to gain from mimicking spit. But, they're not. However, an insect, conveniently named the spittlebug, is responsible for saliva-covered plant stems.

Frog spit is an almost appropriate description as spittlebugs belong to a group of insects also known as the froghoppers. Adult spittlebugs, you see, look like quarter-inch long Kermits. Just as some butterfly larvae look like feces, it is the young froghoppers that generate the spit.

How? Therein lies a tale which begins at the larva's tail end. Froghopper eggs typically hatch in mid-May. The tiny moist larva wastes no time inserting its hypodermic-like proboscis into nearby plant tissue so that it can suck out the juices. It is as the plant sap is extruded that the spittle is formed.

As the larva secretes a mixture of goo and air out of its anus, the bug moves its body up and down in a billow-like motion. A combination of tail wagging, bubble blowing, and hind leg manipulating arranges the bubbles securely around the spittlebug.

Why go to all this trouble to produce clumps of spittle? First, as mentioned above, the froghopper larvae are moist and it is thought that the spittle keeps them from drying out. Second, the spit enclosure is thought to insulate its occupant from extremes of heat or cold. Finally and most importantly, it is a deterrent to predators. If you were a bug muncher, you'd have to suck a lot of spit to get to the chewy center.

Just under two dozen species of spittlebugs can be found in the Great Lakes states. The common one in this area is the meadow spittlebug. Although it might upset your sense of aesthetics, it rarely causes any significant damage. Should you apply an insecticide, guess what will protect the spittlebug larva from the chemical spray?

That's right, its luxuriously thick coat of drivel.

Spitting for Luck

Spit wasn't always thought to be disgusting. Among the ancient Greeks and Romans, spit was considered a good luck charm. People might spit for luck on a found coin; traders spit on the first money earned in the day; boxers spit on their hands. That being the case, go for an early summer walk in a grassy natural area. There is plenty of lucky froghopper spittle for all of you.

SEX AND THE SINGLE FIREFLY

Two by two and side by side
Love's gonna find you yes it is
You just can't hide

—Seth Justman & Peter Wolf (J. Geils Band)

Often I open these articles with some quaint quotation from bygone days. Not this time, not with lightning bugs. Nope, this story calls for rock'n'roll.

But first, when it comes to fireflies, we first need to do some entomological house cleaning.

None of the Above

For the record, fireflies or lightning bugs are neither. True flies (Order Diptera) have only one pair of wings. "Fireflies" have four wings.

True bugs (Order Hemiptera) also have two pairs of wings. The base of the front wings are thickened and leathery while the tail end is membranous. This is not so with "lightning bugs."

A lightning bug is actually a very soft-bodied beetle that looks like it has had its head removed.

You see, all insects have three major body parts: a head at one end, a thorax in the middle (where the legs and wings are attached), and an abdomen at the other end.

Fireflies appear to have only two body parts. In fact, the head is hiding under the "shield" covering the thorax.

Yellows & Greens

I've had the blues
The reds and the pinks
One thing for sure
Love stinks

Obviously, fireflies are most easily identified by their flashing tail lights. This light is produced in an amazingly efficient matter.

The yellow, greenish, or bluish light emitted by lightning bugs is produced by the oxidation of a substance called luciferin. Ninety-eight percent of the energy produced by this chemical reaction is given off as light while only two percent is lost as heat.

By controlling the delivery of oxygen to the light-producing organs, the firefly regulates its flashing.

While some other insects glow, only a firefly can turn its light on and off in a distinct pattern. The pattern is key as each species has it own flashing rhythm.

The male of one species, for example, flashes his beetle beacon every 5.8 seconds. Essentially, he's introducing himself and is looking for a female of his species to flash him back.

It is not only the interval between these mating signals that can separate species but also the color, duration, intensity, grouping, and distance flown between flashes.

As you watch this tiny fireworks display on a quiet summer evening, you may notice that some of the flashers stay down in the grass. These are probably females since, in some species, the females are wingless. Some folks refer to these grounded girls as glowworms.

Should a male find a responsive female, more signals and responses complete this bioluminescent courtship. Soon he will land, they will mate, and she will stop signaling unless…

Femme Fatale

> *You love her*
> *But she loves him*
> *And he loves somebody else*
> *You just can't win*
> *And so it goes*
> *Till the day you die*

… unless she is a female from a species that can change her flashing pattern. Why would she do this? It's called aggressive mimicry and here's how it works.

You've mated and you're hungry. There's no need to attract another male for breeding purposes. Over your head horny guys from other species are displaying their luminous mating signals.

You respond with a species appropriate mating pattern and down they fly excitedly lighting their little love lamps… for the last time. *Bon appetit!*

Yes, fireflies are carnivorous. Besides other insects, fireflies will eat snails, slugs, and other small ground creatures.

Summer's Arrival

After a long cold winter, the first signs of spring, be it a opening crocus or a calling red-winged blackbird, are noted with much anticipation.

Spring may be warmly welcomed (pun intended) but it is a hectic season. Birds have to mate and migrate NOW! Forest flowers have to grow and blossom NOW! The grass has to be mowed and the garden planted NOW!

Signs of summer's arrival are, like the season, a bit more slow and subtle. The first quiet flashing of a firefly counts as one of my clues that summer is upon us.

You may wonder where the lightning bugs came from? In fact, they are here all year. They spend the winter as larvae burrowed in the ground. In spring, they emerge and feed, often in swampy or wet areas. Later in spring they pupate in an earthen cell arriving as adults usually in June.

Fireflies may put on a show for us in summer but when it comes to our local weather extremes, they've been through it all which brings me back to our rock song.

With apologies to the J. Geils band, I've taken a few liberties with the words in the last stanza of their classic tune, *Love Stinks.*

I've flown by diamonds
I've crawled on minks
I've been through it all
Love blinks.

GRASSHOPPERS: The Long & Short of It

Every autumn, second grade classes from the local school district visit our nature center. The classes are studying insects and almost every student gets a close look at a grasshopper. So let's join them and take a close look at two types of grasshoppers commonly found in our area.

Katydids and Locusts

This is not complicated. If a grasshopper has slender antennae that are longer than its body, it is a long-horned grasshopper. Katydids, for example, are long-horned grasshoppers.

If the antennae are much shorter than its body, it is a short-horned grasshopper. Some types of short-horned grasshoppers are known as locusts. All grasshoppers, and crickets for that matter, belong to an Order of insects called Orthoptera, meaning straight-winged. This certainly describes short-horned grasshoppers. At rest, their outer wings run straight along their bodies. In comparison, long-horned grasshoppers hold their wings in more of a tent-like fashion.

Both types of grasshoppers spend their winters as eggs. Katydids lay their eggs in plant tissue while short-horned grasshoppers lay their eggs in the ground.

Speaking of eggs, female long-horned grasshoppers are equipped with long, swordlike ovipositors which is a fancy word for egg layers. These little harmless swords, mounted at the end of the abdomen, can be quite noticeable. Female locusts, on the other hand, have blunt-tipped tail ends.

Long and short-horned grasshoppers have well-developed compound eyes and chewing mouthparts. They also have large, muscular hind legs that are used for more than just jumping.

Grasshopper Summerfest

What's a summer festival without music? When it comes to the sounds of summer, grasshoppers really get the joint jumping, so to speak.

Grasshoppers produce incessant, pitchless almost mechanical sounds. Most short-horned hoppers do this by rubbing a series of projections on those large hind legs against a scraper on its wings. Long-horned grasshoppers strum a scraper on one wing across a file-like ridge on the other wing.

When it comes to the festival's food booths, grasshoppers will be lining up for vegetarian fare. If times are tough due to drought or overpopulation, grasshoppers can become scavengers, carnivores, or even cannibals.

Common Meadow Katydid (*Orchelimum vulgare*)

Now, let's zoom in on one example of each type of grasshopper. We'll start with the common meadow katydid (see page 25). They are about 1.25 inches long with a green body and pale brown legs. This color scheme helps camouflage them in their preferred habitats of fields and low meadows.

A female meadow katydid, which is larger than the males, is choosy about where it lays its eggs. She will chew test holes in several stems before turning around and inserting her eggs in the hole. When done, she'll turn around and chew the hole shut.

In the winter, little meadow katydid nymphs stay dormant in their eggs waiting for late spring to emerge. They will shed their skins several times before becoming adults in late July.

Katydid growth is fueled by eating a wide variety of plants. They have also been known to eat moths, soldier beetles, and other katydids.

Many insectivores dine on katydids. A partial list would include other insects, frogs, snakes, small mammals, spiders, and birds.

Red-legged Grasshopper (*Melanoplus femurrubrum*)

This inch-long locust can be difficult to identify since it comes in shades of green, yellow, red-brown, and dark brown.

The hind legs are, indeed, red or yellowish. If you have one in hand, the black herringbone pattern on the femurs is quite distinctive.

If you do have one in hand, you are also likely to be stained by "tobacco juice," digestive juices produced by the grasshopper to discourage predators. Not to worry, this juice is harmless to us.

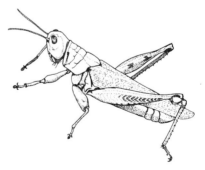

They would rather escape their enemies by flying which, much to the dismay of a net-wielding child, they are quite good at. Red-legged grasshoppers can cover up to forty feet in one flight, usually about three feet above the vegetation.

Speaking of vegetation, the list of their food plants is extensive including sweetclover, goldenrods, chicory, ragweed, dandelion, vetches, trefoils, plus a variety of grasses. Farmers are not too fond of this locust as they also eat alfalfa, soybeans, oats, corn, cabbage, and potatoes.

Biblical Plagues?

...they shall be afraid of that which is high, and terrors shall be in the way... and the grasshopper shall be a burden, and desire shall fail; because man goeth to his everlasting home...

—Ecclesiastes 12:5

My my, that doesn't sound too good for the grasshopper what with that everlasting home and all. You see, some species of short-horned grasshoppers, known as the plague locusts, have solitary and gregarious phases. The latter form huge "clouds" that can number into the tens to hundreds of millions.

These species are generalist feeders and can devour hundreds of square miles of crops. Keep in mind that they aren't specializing in crop plants; they are just taking advantage of a conveniently concentrated food source.

To put these locust numbers in perspective, let's review the food chain courtesy of textbook author G. Tyler Miller, Jr.: "One hundred trout are needed to support one man for a year. The trout, in turn, must consume 90,000 frogs, that must consume 27 million grasshoppers that live off of 1,000 tons of grass."

Luckily for us, the worst of these plague locusts live in northern Africa. It is understandable that early civilizations came to fear these swarms of hungry locusts and thought of them as a punishment imposed by a wrathful god.

Sunday School Spirits

Grasshoppers are used elsewhere in religious teachings. With that in mind, I thought this last story might be of interest.

A minister was teaching his fifth grade Sunday school class about the life of John the Baptist. He told how John had lived in the wilderness with little to eat besides honey and locusts.

A little girl asked what locusts are. The minister said, "A locust is a grasshopper." The little girl responded, "Oh, my grandmother *drinks* those."

WOOLLY BEARS & GUEST GNATS

Every year, usually around mid-October, one of the students visiting the nature center turns up a woolly bear caterpillar (*Pyrrharctia isabella)*. This always brings a smile to my face because this is the first bug I can remember keeping in a jar. In fact, my sister reminded me of an old family film where I (a 3-year-old larva) am mesmerized by a woolly bear crawling on a twig.

As I grew up and learned more about butterflies and moths, the more I realized how curious it is to find a caterpillar so late in the season.

You see, some butterflies and moths spend the winters in cocoons or chrysalids, others as an egg, but the woolly bear spends the winter as a woolly bear curled up under a rock or log. It's a good thing they're wearing such a nice fur coat.

For those who may not have seen this familiar larva, it is black at both ends and brownish red in the middle. In October, the inch-and-a-half long caterpillar can often be seen scurrying across roads and paths searching for a rock, flower pot, or a log to crawl under for the winter.

Once there, woolly bears can virtually freeze solid withstanding temperatures as low as 20°F. They do this with help of glycerol, a sort of anti-freeze for biological tissues.

Winter Forecaster?

One of the popular myths about how severe a winter will be relates to the woolly bear. Allegedly, the wider the red band, the worse winter will be. In fact, the wider the red band, the older the caterpillar. It's kind of like gray hair.

In the first three to four weeks of their lives, they undergo six molts, shedding their outer skin and hair as they grow larger. After each molt, the red band increases in size.

This classic black-and-red model is the larva of the Isabella Tiger Moth. They feed on common plantain, dandelion, aster, clover, burdock and other common plants.

The caterpillar spotters among you (both of you) might be thinking, "Wait a second, I've seen ones that look more like a blonde than a redhead or a brunette."

These are different species of tiger moths, such as the yellow woolly bear or the dogbane tiger moth. The larva of the latter, as its name suggests, dines on dogbane.

Yellow woolly bears can be found chewing on a variety of tree leaves, from cherries and maples to walnuts and willows.

When disturbed, all of these furry caterpillars curl into a ball and can be remarkably slippery when you try to pick one up.

Other Winter Bugs

So, now that the woolly bears are under a board or a piece of bark, where are some of our other bugs this winter?

Some butterflies, such as the mourning cloak, actually spend the winter as a butterfly. They seek out a secluded spot such as a tree hollow. I remember seeing one at the peak of a lean-to located along a cross-country ski trail in central Minnesota. I was skiing at the time and just shook my head at this tough little critter ... no gore tex, polypropylene or anything.

While at the tree, look at the ground near its base. At such a spot, you might notice something that looks like fine coffee grounds hopping around on the snow. These are snow fleas. No, they are not true fleas like you might find on a pet but rather belong to a group of tiny insects called springtails. Millions of these miniature vegetarians can be found on a single acre.

Other tiny winter bugs are living inside a custom-built house, known as gall, grown by a plant. A gall is caused when an insect secretes a chemical that causes a plant to grow in an aberrant manner. Insect galls can be found on a variety of plants.

Here at Stillman, some of my favorites galls, which look like pine cones, are found at the tips of willows branches. The occupant is the larva of a small gnat, also called a midge, which is just two tenths of an inch long.

Although the midge triggered the gall to grow, other bugs will share the accommodations. For example, species of "guest gnats" will move in. (I bet you've had some guest gnats over at your house during the holiday season.)

You're Only Young Once

While writing this article and looking for six-legged ideas, one of our nature center's Board members brought me a woolly bear from her window well. I wanted to get this little guy back in an appropriate winter dormitory as soon as possible.

Coincidentally, it was my birthday. While driving back to the nature center, I thought about the family movie my sister described. I put the woolly bear in a small pile of logs. With any luck, at least one of us will mature.

TREES

Osage oranges. Photo by Mark Spreyer.

III. TREES

The tree which moves some to tears of joy is in the eyes of others only a green thing that stands in the way. Some see nature all ridicule and deformity...and some scarce see nature at all.
But to the eyes of the man of imagination, nature is imagination itself.

—William Blake

SUGAR MAPLE: Service with a Spile

The land-holder who appropriates a few rods of land to the preservation or cultivation of the sugar tree not only increases the value of his estate, but confers a benefit upon future generations.

—Supt. of the 1860 U.S. Census

My first permanent job as a naturalist was at a New York nature center that tapped maple trees as an educational program and sold the syrup to raise funds. As my career progressed, I continued to drill holes in maples whether they grew in Illinois or in the suburbs of Minneapolis. So, it's no surprise that I'm an unabashed sugar maple enthusiast.

Part of the fun of tapping sugar maples is that it gets you outside just as spring is getting underway. The best weather for collecting sap is when the days are above freezing while nighttime temperatures drop below freezing. Around here, that's usually late February through much of March.

Since sugar maple is an indigenous tree, maple syrup and sugar are North American products. Native Americans introduced us to this wonderful treat. There are various legends about how the Indians learned about maple sap. In my favorite version, a brave was taking a nap under a tree when his wife brought over a cooking pot, a not-so-subtle hint that he should get some water. Not about to do "woman's work," the man threw his tomahawk into the tree and stormed off. Sap soon dripped from the axe into the bowl beneath.

When his wife returned for the pot, she saw that it was full of "water" and used it to cook stew. When husband and wife got together for dinner, they discovered, much to their delight, that the meat was covered in a sweet and tasty sauce.

Early in the 19th century, the movement to abolish the slave trade found a friend in maple sugar. In his 1824 *Compendium of Agriculture,* William Drown wrote, "The cane sugar is the result of the forced labor of the most wretched slaves, toiling under the cruel lash of a cutting whip. While the maple sugar is made by those who are happy and free."

A Two-bit Operation

Of course, tapping maples with tomahawks is hard on the trees. Nowadays, we use a brace and either a 3/8" or 7/16" bit. You only need to drill a hole two to three inches in and at a downward pitch. Remember, a tappable maple ideally is larger than ten inches in diameter at breast height. Next, you need a spile or a tap. These can be purchased from a specialty supplier or fashioned from a sumac twig.

Buckets are the time-honored way of collecting sap although any container such as plastic bags or milk jugs can be used. If you are using a small container, you will need to check them often as a good tree will fill it quickly. How much sap do you need? A lot. You can figure 35 - 50 gallons of sap for one gallon of syrup or eight pounds of sugar. Most trees will produce ten to twelve gallons of sap during the season.

One of the reasons genuine maple syrup is so expensive is that it takes a great deal of energy to boil the sap down to the consistency of syrup. Sap averages 1-3% sugar while syrup is 65% sugar. It takes about five hours to boil down five gallons of sap.

As you can imagine, the process produces a great deal of steam. If you try it indoors, be warned— keep your windows open or an exhaust fan going. If you don't, kiss your wallpaper goodbye!

Good & Bad News

In regards to the Stillman Nature Center and syrup, I've got good news and bad news. First, the bad news. Whoever owned this property back in 1860 did not follow the advice of the Superintendent of the 1860 U.S. Census given at the top of this story. So, this "future generation" is not benefiting.

This brings us to the good news. To honor a former Stillman board member, a local garden club arranged to have two sugar maples donated to Stillman.

As these maples are only a few inches in diameter, it will be quite a while before we can tap them. Since I'll be retired (or worse) before Stillman's maples can be tapped for syrup, I'm going to drown my sorrows with another fine North American product, Tennessee whiskey. After all, sugar maple charcoal is used to mellow Jack Daniels.

WALNUTS FOR THE LONG RUN

When I first came to Stillman Nature Center, I could only find one walnut (*Juglans nigra*) tree of any size. Its trunk was about as big around as an arm. This situation needed to be corrected.

Tireless volunteer Roger Laegeler had a friend who collected bags of walnuts. Roger, in turn, brought them to Stillman.

More Than One Nut Loose

Then, I had the great fun of doing my version of Johnny Appleseed, Mark the Walnut Chucker. I'd walk or ride the mower down the trails, tossing some walnuts to my left, chucking some to my right, flinging them in all directions.

At first, my training as a forester made me a bit more judicious in choosing the locations for my walnut dispersal activities. One day, though, I had left a couple of bags of walnuts in the garage with the door open.

After pausing to answer the phone, I came out only to discover that an entrepreneurial squirrel had decided to open a bag and go into the walnut business for itself. Seeing this reminded me that where I placed the walnuts and where they finally ended up was not in my control.

Since I have become the squirrels' silent partner in the walnut distribution business, young walnuts have started sprouting in various locations around Stillman.

Walnuts have a large pinnately (feather-like) compound leaf

made up of 15 – 23 leaflets (see illustration). Each leaflet can be up to 1.5 inches wide and 3.5 inches long. Put 15 – 23 of those together and you've got one big leaf!

This brings me back to that first walnut tree. Recently, I noticed that some of the immature nuts had been knocked loose during a strong storm. By the way, walnut trees are very resistant to storm damage.

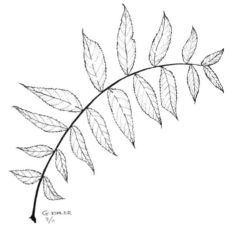

Walnuts do not fall from a tree ready to crack open. No, they are covered with a light green, aromatic, somewhat roughened husk.

The aroma is distinctive and anything but subtle. Dig your fingernail into that green hull and you will be rewarded with a refreshing mix of citrus and spice. Be advised that the husk contains a brown dye that can stain your hand.

Inside the husk and a protective shell that requires cracking is the tasty kernel that most people, especially those who cook, are familiar with.

Keep in mind that many walnuts used in the kitchen are English walnuts (*Juglans regia*) that are grown in this country but are indigenous to southeastern Europe and Asia.

CSI: Walnut Grove

In addition to producing desirable fruit, black walnut is the most valuable timber tree in eastern North America. It is a favorite of furniture makers. The wood is a rich chocolate color with a beautifully figured grain.

Its value was not lost on early colonists. As early as 1610, black walnut was being exported from Virginia back to England.

Today, superior black walnut trees are being poached by unethical loggers. In one Indiana case, an incensed landowner called his state's Department of Natural Resources to report a stolen black walnut tree. All that was left was some chainsawed branches and a stump.

Two large walnut logs, that appeared to match the stump, were discovered at a saw mill about 60 miles away. To positively confirm these were the stolen logs, scientists from Purdue University were contacted.

Thanks to DNA fingerprinting, the suspect logs matched the stump with such a high degree of accuracy that the lumber poachers had to pay a sizable fine to the landowner. In this case, CSI stands for Crime Stem Investigation.

Competition & Allelopathy

While illegal logging can cause trees to disappear, walnut trees can keep other plants from ever appearing. This is done via a natural process known as allelopathy

Remember, it's a dogwood eat dogwood world out there. Nearby plants are all competing for sunlight, water, and nutrients. Wouldn't it be advantageous if the number of competitors was restricted?

That's where allelopathy comes in. Allelopathy is a way of preventing competitors from entering the contest.

With black walnut, allelopathy involves the secretion of a biochemical, juglone, into the soil that inhibits the growth of some types of surrounding vegetation. Juglone can be found in the tree's roots, buds, seed hulls, and leaves. In particular, walnut seedlings, tomatoes, plus some conifers and fruit trees don't do well under walnuts.

A wide variety of other plants, everything from daylilies to redbud trees, can grow near walnut trees. Some plants, such as Kentucky bluegrass, actually seem to do better near walnuts.

Speaking of bluegrass, it has allelopathic tendencies of its own. Other allelopathic plants include sugar maple, hackberry, bracken fern, mesquite, garlic mustard, and some oaks. When put in perspective, the allelopathic rap against walnuts is a bit overblown.

About Last Night...

Enough about lumber and biochemistry. Let's get back to the tree. Speaking from experience with that first Stillman walnut tree, I know that many years can pass before a young walnut tree starts to produce nuts. Compared to some fruit trees, walnuts are not in a hurry to reproduce.

However, the tree is home to a nocturnal species whose entire adult life is devoted to mating. I'm speaking of the luna moth. This is one large and unmistakable moth. It is pale green in color with a wingspan of four to five inches. Each hind wing sports a long tail while the leading margins of the forewings are purplish red.

It is this moth's chunky green caterpillar that chows down on walnut leaves. When the adult moth emerges from its cocoon, however, it will never eat again. The luna moth doesn't have a functional mouth. Its simple purpose is to fly at night and mate.

All of which sets up the first two stanzas from Robert Crawford's marvelous poem *Luna Moth*.

> *Although I can't know what the now*
> *Of moths without a mouth might be,*
> *I hope they are content with how*
> *Design ensures posterity:*
> *The organ of their larval duty—*
> *Consuming every leaf in sight—*
> *Effaced for purposes of beauty*
> *That serves a different appetite.*

It makes me wonder, could allelopathic and aphrodisiac compounds be one in the same?

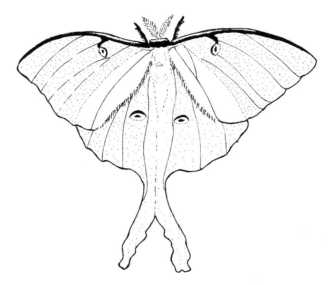

THE SECRET OF ASH-LEAVED MAPLE

There is no better time to appreciate trees than fall. The sugar and red maples, for example, put on quite a show. Some maples are not as poplar, I mean, popular as their colorful cousins. In this article, I'd like to concentrate on the ash-leaved maple, one of the lesser-known trees.

Like all maples, ash-leaved maples have opposite leaves. In other words, the leaves are arranged in pairs, like arms and legs. Unlike other maples, ash-leaved maples have compound leaves. Compound leaves are made up of leaflets; in ash-leaved maple's case, three to seven leaflets.

Now, guess what other local tree has opposite compound leaves? That's right, ash. Ash leaves, though, typically have seven to nine leaflets.

While recognizing leaves is a useful means of identifying trees, botanists organize plants by their flowers which, of course, develop into seeds. Simply put, all oaks have acorns and all maples have "helicopters" or double samaras, if you want to get technical. Ash trees have single samaras that resemble tiny canoe paddles (see inside back cover).

Each maple species' helicopter has a distinctive configuration. Compare, for example, ash-leaved maple to sugar maple.

Home, Home on the Range... Almost Any Range
Ash-leaved maple's helicopters are familiar to many because this maple is a widespread species. It can be found growing from

Vermont across to Alberta, down to Texas and through the southern states back to Florida. Its presence in the north-central part of the continent earned it another common name, Manitoba maple.

Although the tree prefers moist soils, it can also grow on poorer sites. It is, in fact, one of the most adaptable members of the maple clan. Early settlers in the Midwest and Great Plains were acquainted with ash-leaved maple's hardiness, especially in extremes of climate, and planted it widely around their homesteads and villages.

While ash-leaved maple is short-lived (75 - 100 years), it grows fast. A sapling can grow two feet or more in a year. In just a few years, pioneers, or their livestock, could enjoy a shaded doorway or drinking trough.

If these settlers had moved from the eastern U.S., where sugar maple grows, they were probably quick to discover that a milder version of maple syrup could be produced from Manitoba maple's sap. Plains Indian Tribes, such as the Crow, certainly knew how to make sugar from the tree. Is it any wonder that yet another common name for this tree is sugar ash?

On a personal note, I can vouch for the subtle sweetness of Manitoba maple syrup. My career has taken me from New York to Minnesota. It was in New York that I first learned how to tap sugar maples and boil the sap down to syrup. It is a time and firewood-consuming process, but absolutely nothing beats the flavor of true maple syrup.

Later in Minnesota, while working at a nature center along the Mississippi River, ash-leaved maples were all around. Not surprisingly, we tapped those trees. It took more firewood to boil it down, but the syrup was still vastly superior to the simulated maple syrups for sale in most grocery stores.

Where the Deer and the Cecropia Play

While rarely planted by today's human homeowners, ash-leaved maple continues to provide food and housing for birds, mammals, and insects.

Grosbeaks, grouse, quail, nuthatches plus chipmunks and squirrels all enjoy the seeds. A wide variety of wildlife use the trees for cover or as nesting sites.

As for insects, the star of the Manitoba maple stage is undoubtedly the cecropia moth. This spectacular moth is probably the best known moth species on the continent. Its wings, which are 4.25 to 6 inches across, have the largest surface area of all the moths in this region.

It is the cecropia larva that feeds on ash-leaved maple leaves. The thick green caterpillar grows to four inches in length and is decorated with pairs of red, orange and yellow tubercles.

Thinking Outside the Box

By now, some of you may have guessed that the *secret* of ash-leaved maple, aka Manitoba maple, aka sugar ash, is that it is better known as boxelder (*Acer negundo*). I can hear you now, "That's a trash tree and what about those boxelder bugs?"

What about 'em? Do they sting you? No. Do they harm your house? No. Do they feed on your flowers? No. What they do feed on is the flowers of the female boxelder.

Yes, there are male and female ash-leaved maples. Interestingly, nature has a way of sorting the genders out. Females are often found along streams, while male boxelders are more likely to be growing on drier upland sites. By selecting male boxelders for your yard, you can avoid the harmless boxelder bugs and the helicopters.

If I haven't convinced you yet that ash-leaved maple deserves a place on your property, consider the following four reasons: oak wilt, Dutch elm disease, bronze birch borer, and emerald ash borer. As these diseases and insects decimate our yards and urban forests, there's at least one tree that will still provide shade and homes for colorful wildlife.

One Person's Trash...

In her wonderful 2006 book, *Bird-by-Bird Gardening*, Sally Roth comments on "trash trees" such as "...poplars, hackberries, boxelders, and other trees that spring up in unattended areas almost as soon as your back is turned."

She continues with a description of her yard in Indiana:

One of my most successful bird gardens was a 6-foot-wide strip that we simply stopped mowing along one side of our country yard...chokecherries, wild plums, and lots of other fast-growing native trees— 'weeds', in other words— sprang up and grew like lightning. In just a few years, I had a great natural hedgerow that was burgeoning with vireos, flycatchers, orioles, bluebirds, wrens, robins, flickers, native sparrows, even quail.
Trash trees? I don't think such a thing exists. Trees that volunteer, grow 6 feet tall in a year or two, and provide super bird appeal are more like true treasure.

COTTONWOOD COUNTRY

Let me be by myself in the evenin' breeze
Listen to the murmur of the cottonwood trees
Send me off forever but I ask you please
Don't fence me in

—Cole Porter

Don't Fence Me In was quite a popular song, particularly with the singing cowboys, in the mid-twentieth century. When you stop to think about it, it is not the only time that cottonwood trees appear in song lyrics. If you haven't stopped to think about it, now's the time.

Murmuring in the Breeze

Eastern cottonwood (*Populus deltoides*) has a very descriptive scientific name. As you might guess, *populus* is Latin for people. So, we are talking about the people's tree.

In addition to indigenous species, many cultivated varieties of *Populus* have been planted across the U. S. You might say, poplars are popular.

The species name *Deltoides* stems, if you will, from the triangular Greek letter delta. The cottonwood's leaf is triangular as well. It is the stem of the leaf, called a petiole, which explains why the cottonwood turns up in many songs.

With inspiration from Cole Porter, picture yourself

hiking alone on a beautiful spring evening. You pause on a bridge over a small stream. Along its banks grow elms, maples, and cottonwoods.

A slight breeze moves through the trees. If you're a songwriter, you likely enjoy the cottonwoods' restful whispers.

If you're a student of nature, you might wonder why, in comparison, are the elm and maple leaves so quiet? All you have to do is collect a leaf from each tree and the answer will be in your hand.

Most petioles are rounded and somewhat stiff. Some, like the elm's, are very short. A light breeze quietly passes around leaves attached in such a way.

The leaf stem on a cottonwood is quite a different matter. It is long, flexible and flattened at a right angle to the surface of the leaf.

The least puff of wind catches these petioles like little sails and sets the leaf to quivering. Other poplars also have vertically flattened leaf stems. Now you know why quaking aspen (*Populus tremuloides*) quakes.

Male Call

> *I love to see the cottonwood blossom*
> *In the early spring*
> *I love to see the message of love*
> *That the bluebird brings*

These cheery opening lines written by De Lange, Loesser, and Meyer are setting you up for disappointment. After all, the song is titled *I Wish I Were Blind.*

I suppose one could say the same about cottonwood blossoms. They are a spring delight that later leads to mounds of wind-blown fluff, that some find annoying.

Of course, not all cottonwood trees produce the seeds that earned this tree its common name. You see, there are male and female cottonwood trees, and male trees do not produce seed.

The pendulous male catkins, a type of flower, are three to four inches long and decorated with red anthers (where the pollen is made).

Female flowers are shorter and greenish-yellow in color. Compared to the male catkins, the female flowers are semi-rigid and hang more stiffly from the twig.

By late May, the female flowers have become greenish-brown capsules grouped in elongated clusters, containing numerous seeds with cottony hairs attached. The hairs are there to catch a gust of wind and spread the seeds far and wide, perhaps to an exposed riverside mud flat.

Water & Fire

Out on the trail night birds are callin'
Singing their wild melody
Down in the canyon cottonwood whispers
A Song of Wyoming for me

When Kent Lewis wrote these lyrics in *Song of Wyoming*, he could have been listening to our cottonwood. Eastern cottonwood does range as far west as Montana. That's why it's also known as plains cottonwood. It is in fact the state tree of Wyoming, Kansas, and Nebraska. Regardless of the state, cottonwoods are often found growing by a river or a lake.

If you are growing in a plains state, being near water is a good place for a thirsty tree to be. Cottonwoods are designed to collect rain water and hold fast against prairie winds.

They have a shallow, widespread root system sprouting numerous fine rootlets. This system combines to absorb surface water, hold soil, and make the tree wind-firm.

As you probably know, prairie winds power grassland fires. Larger cottonwoods are ready for that as well. Obviously, if you are growing in a river floodplain, the odds are low that a fire will reach you.

This is good for the young, small cottonwoods that are vulnerable to fire. However, they aren't small for long. A newly planted cottonwood can grow four to five feet each year.

By the time the tree is twenty years old, its thickly furrowed bark offers some protection from a ground fire. By the way, cottonwoods can live for 100 years and reach a height of 100 feet.

A White Tie Dinner

There's a cottonwood tree with a limb hangin' over
We'll do the cannonball off a rope swing'

Trent Willmon sets this lakeside scene in his song *The Good Life*. What he may not realize is that there are some other lake inhabitants that see cottonwoods as part of their good life. These would be carp.

I kid you not. I first ran across this fact decades ago in *Fishing for Buffalo*, a book dedicated to the joys of angling for roughfish. Rob Buffler, one of the authors, recalled, "I was fishing a lake west of Minneapolis in the late '70s when I saw a carp taking cottonwood seeds off the surface."

He was not the only one to connect carp and cottonwoods. In a 2005 story for *Pennsylvania Angler & Boater*, Carl Haensel described catching a carp with a cottonwood fly. He concluded the article with detailed instructions on how to tie a cottonwood fly.

The next time you're sweeping the cottonwood fluff off your steps, think about this. Somewhere some guy is using cell foam and turkey down to make an imitation cottonwood seed puff!

Screen Stars

I understand there are some people who have considered cutting down cottonwood trees because they don't like the mess, particularly in window screens. Talk about throwing the baby out with the bath, I mean, river water! Here's an idea. Take down your screens, plug in the vacuum cleaner, and... suck it up!

Remember the Arapaho believed great cottonwoods cast the stars into the heavens. So no, those aren't annoying seeds, they're potential stars.

BLACK CHERRY: A WILDLIFE CORNUCOPIA

Life has a way of coming full circle. My life-long curiosity about nature began through exploring my family's property that is just a couple of miles from the Stillman Nature Center. I clearly recall, although it happened decades ago, collecting the most fantastic looking caterpillar, a sort of animated art deco toothbrush, from a tree that grew by the lake in the backyard.

Later, I watched a catbird, a bird that mimics the calls of other birds, feeding on the berries from this same tree. The tree, I later learned, was a black cherry which provides food to approximately 100 species of wildlife plus over 200 species of butterflies and moths, including the white-marked tussock moth whose caterpillar I had kept in a jar.

Drinking Clubs & Cherry Bears

As a forestry student in Michigan's Upper Peninsula, I was no longer caging caterpillars, but the wildlife benefits of black cherries surrounded me. Take an early summer walk down a primitive logging road, for example. During such an outing, it was not uncommon to come across a dozen or more tiger swallowtails, collected around a puddle. When disturbed, these butterfly "drinking clubs" would become a surreal cloud of yellow-and-black. What is one of the principal food plants for tiger swallowtail caterpillars? You guessed it, black cherry.

Later in the summer, on these same forest roads, I would notice that young cherry trees, with stems the size of broom handles, had apparently fallen or been blown into the road. On closer examination, you could see that these skinny-yet-tall trees had actually been pushed down by black bears. You see, the bears wanted the cherries and the trees were just too spindly to climb. As you might imagine, those who grow domesticated cherries aren't too fond of these "cherry bears."

At the turn of this century, I taught college courses such as a Wildlife Resource Management class. As I review my lecture notes, it's amazing how many times planting cherry trees was recommended as a way to encourage wild birds and animals.

If you want to attract wildlife to your yard, growing cherry trees can be easy to do. In fact, because so many birds eat cherries and spread their seeds, you might already have a black cherry tree growing along a fence line or in a forgotten corner of your lot.

The following clues will help you identify this tree. Black cherry has elliptical leaves, with a pointed tip, that are 2 - 5 inches long and about a third as wide. They are shiny dark green above, lighter below, with fine teeth along the edge. A pair of red glands can be found on the leaf stem and reddish hairs line the midvein beneath.

Young trees have smooth, dark reddish brown bark marked with conspicuous, horizontal lenticels. Lenticels are small areas of loose tissue that appear as dots, warts or short lines. The bark on older and larger trees is rough, blackish and broken into thick irregular plates. It always reminds me of burnt potato chips.

Dining and Dying on Cherry

Speaking of chips, this tree feeds humans as well as birds. Jelly and wine are prepared from the fruit and a cough medicine, wild cherry syrup, is obtained from the bark. In fact, this native cherry has been valued by nonnative Europeans almost as soon as they arrived on this continent. Its valuable wood was used for furniture, paneling, handles and toys. Black cherry was one of the first New World trees brought to England to enhance their gardens. Such a transatlantic transplant was recorded as early as 1629.

Making furniture from black cherry is not as easy as it was in years gone by. By the end of the 19th century, hardwood buyers were searching the country for high quality cherry trees. They did their job well as most of the remaining wild cherries are limby or short-trunked. However, this doesn't mean they can't be utilized.

Back in the 90's, I was having lunch with Ray, a local acquaintance and Barrington resident, and he showed me pictures of a charming cherry dining room table and hutch. He had fashioned this furniture from wild cherry trees that had grown along a fence line on his property.

This property was his father's before him. I imagine he knew these cherries throughout his life. They were dying when he cut them. As a woodworker, Ray just couldn't stand watching this beautiful wood rot away. Some might object that he denied animals a room in the "dead cherry tree *hole*-tel." Given the many trees he has planted on his lot, I'm sure the woodpeckers didn't miss the cherries.

These trees fed many generations of birds and caterpillars before Ray and his family began to feed off the surface of the cherry table. Ray's work reminded me of a story about the elder Daniel Boone. It is reported that Boone made himself several cherry caskets, and would occasionally sleep in them in his old age. He gave away all but his last to needy corpses. Life and cherry trees do have a way of coming full circle.

OSAGE ORANGE: History in its Roots

They are called hedge apples, hedge balls, mock oranges, and, my favorite, green brain (see page 54). The citrus-smelling fruit of the osage orange tree does bear a striking resemblance to hardened, green brains.

Hedge apple is also an appropriate name because this native of Texas, Arkansas and Oklahoma was spread to Illinois and beyond by farmers who valued the tree as an important component of a living fence. So when you see one around here, it's a reminder of our bygone farming heritage.

However, this small tree has played a much larger role in history. With that in mind, let's leave the irresistible fruit behind and take a look at the osage orange's roots, so to speak.

Lewis and Clark

Over two hundred years ago, one of the most amazing explorations in human history took place, Lewis and Clark's Corps of Discovery. The first tree they sent back east from St. Louis was the osage orange.

Osage refers to the Indian tribe that lived near the home range of the tree. Native Americans prized the tree's limber branches for the construction of bows. Because of this, the French termed it *bois d'arc* (wood of the bow). Southerners have transformed the French term to bodark.

Speaking of French, take a look at the tree's scientific name, *Maclura pomifera*. The species name, *pomifera,* should remind you of the French word for apple, *pomme*. The genus name, *maclura*, honors William Maclure (1763-1840), the father of American geology and one of the founding members of the Academy of Natural Sciences in Philadelphia.

As a scientist, I'm sure he would appreciate that the osage orange is a close relative of the mulberries. If you like, just think of hedge apples as hard, soft-ball sized mulberries.

Now what behemoth could swallow hedge apples like a raccoon eats mulberries? How about a mastodon? In fact, 100,000 years ago osage oranges grew as far north as Minnesota and probably served as food for super-sized (now extinct) North American mammals such as mastodons.

Ortho orange?

O.K., so we're back to the hedge balls. It has long been believed having this fruit in your basement or cupboards will discourage unwanted bugs, such as cockroaches, from moving in. One pair of authors dismissed this folklore by writing that osage oranges would only kill a roach "if they happen to fall directly on one."

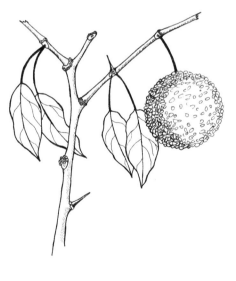

Not so fast fellas. According to research conducted at Iowa State University and presented at a National Meeting of the American Chemical Society, surfaces treated with chemicals produced by osage orange did, indeed, repel cockroaches. Graduate research assistant Chris Peterson observed that "the roaches will venture onto the treated surface, stop, turn around and walk off onto the untreated surface." This research into natural roach repellents seems quite promising.

Back to the Future

So, what does the future hold for this historic tree? Perhaps, it will be grown as a source of insect repellent. I hope so because old osage oranges are getting harder to find. As land becomes more valuable, historic hedgerows, with their osage oranges, are getting bulldozed to make room for a couple more rows of corn or another subdivision.

If you want to grow your own osage orange, one source is American Forests. These folks sell seedlings grown from the national champion, a tree that is over 50 feet tall and 90 feet wide. The champion stands outside the Virginia home of Revolutionary War orator Patrick Henry. It was grown from hedge apples sent back by Lewis and Clark.

Not all hedge apples can trace their roots back to the Corps of Discovery but all serve as reminders of our country's and continent's past. So the next time you drive by an osage orange, think of it as a living historical marker.

THE GINKGO TREE: Planting a Fossil

It's rare that a scientific name for a tree enters the contemporary lexicon but *Ginkgo biloba* certainly has. No, we're not going to discuss how the extract of ginkgo leaves is being used to treat everything from senility to retinopathy. Instead, let's investigate the history of this ancient tree species.

Ginkgo is the only surviving genus of a prehistoric order of plants having characters of both conifers (cone-bearing trees such as pines) and ferns. In fact, another common name for the ginkgo is the maidenhair [fern] tree. The leaflets of the maidenhair fern, which grows here in the Midwest, are smaller but otherwise quite similar to ginkgo leaves.

Ginkgo leaves are unparalleled in the tree world. The veins in a ginkgo leaf, however, are not parallel. Instead, much like a fan, they radiate out from the base of the leaf. Unlike oak or elm leaves, the ginkgo leaf lacks a central vein or midrib. Upon close examination, the ginkgo's fine veins will fork as they approach the leaf's edge.

The species name, *biloba*, refers to the fact that the leaf usually has a narrow notch or sinus that divides the leaf into two lobes. Centuries ago, this lobed look inspired another descriptive name for the ginkgo. The author of the great Chinese Herbal, issued in 1578, calls this tree *Ya-chio-tzu*, which means "the tree with leaves like a duck's foot" (see illustration).

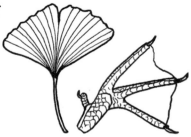

Glacial Globetrotter

As this reference suggests, the ginkgo that has been widely planted in North America originated in China. The ginkgoes brought to this country, after being first brought to Europe, can trace their origins to trees planted in China, Japan or Korea.

It was once thought that none were to be found growing in the 'wild' and, were it not for the arboricultural skills of Buddhist monks, none would have survived. To a certain degree, this is true. Early visitors to the Orient, such as Engelbert Kaempfer, who was the first European to publish an account of the ginkgo, often saw this tree on the grounds of important religious buildings, palaces or tombs. Today, there is good evidence that the ginkgo occurs in a truly wild state in eastern China.

Before the last ice age, when much of Eurasia and North America were buried under glaciers, maidenhair trees could be found growing across the northern hemisphere. It is thought that the glaciers eradicated the species from this continent while a few hung on in Asia.

Given its near global extinction and a revival dependent on human cultivation, you might think the ginkgo is a fragile tree that needs to be handled with care. Nothing could be further from the truth.

While it does grow slowly, it is practically immune to disease and insect pests and is little-harmed by pollutants. Gangly at first, the older ginkgo develops into one of the finest street trees in the temperate world. I don't know about you, but these last two paragraphs give me reason to pause. How is it that a species perfectly suited to an urban landscape evolved during an era when no such landscapes existed? That's a question that remains unanswered. I do know, though, that a wonderful example of a large suburban ginkgo can be seen growing in the parking lot of an chain restaurant at a nearby suburban mall. This gorgeous tree is over 100 years old and is doing well despite having been "malled."

Stinko Ginkgo

The maidenhair tree does have one trait that must be kept in mind, it is a dioecious species. This means that rather than having male and female flowers on the same plant, there are separate male and female trees. The females bear the fruit which gives the tree its name.

Ginkgo is a transliteration of the Chinese symbol of *yin hsing* meaning "silver apricot." Who wouldn't want a tree that bears silver apricots? You wouldn't. Unless, of course, you want a yard full of acrid, putrid-smelling pulp that reminds some of rancid butter and has earned the female tree the nickname "stinko ginkgo." If you choose to plant a ginkgo, make sure it's a male.

O.K., some skeptics are thinking, why would you plant a non-native tree? If you define native as what was growing here in the 19th century, just as Europeans settlers arrived, ginkgoes are non-native. With a smile planted firmly on my face, I would ask, why stop at the 1830s? (The 1830s are when white settlers first started taking root in our area.)

Millennial Mall Meal

If we go way back before any humans arrived on this continent, when dinosaurs were still stumbling into tar pits, the fossil record clearly shows that members of the ginkgo clan thrived in North America. Imagine, for a moment, a pterodactyl perched in the branch of a 100-foot tall ginkgo, searching for easy prey.

Unfortunately, we don't have any dinosaurs to go with our maidenhair trees but if we did.... Well, let's put it this way. If that pterodactyl found itself perched in the restaurant ginkgo, it wouldn't have to look very far for its next snack!

Story Update: Since this article first appeared, the mall ginkgo was cut down.

BIRDS

Woodcock on eggs. Photo by Mark Spreyer.

IV. BIRDS

Birds are, perhaps, the most eloquent expression of reality.

—Roger Tory Peterson

WOODCOCK OBSESSION

You got to love a bird with monikers such as timberdoodle and bogsucker. It is most commonly known as the American woodcock and each spring, it goes through its amazing mating ritual.

While researching this article, I found some old journal entries describing my earliest excursions into the woodcock's world here at the nature center. As you'll read, I also kept an eye and ear out for our local owls.

A woodcock, by the way, is a portly inland sandpiper with a long beak and short legs (see page 84). It is a migratory species that does not return to the area until March.

Also, its mating displays are generally limited to the low-light conditions found on either side of sunset and sunrise. With these facts in mind, here are some edited journal entries from 1986.

March 23

There is still some ice on the pond. Two drakes and one hen mallard are paddling in the open spots.

Friday night, between 11:00 and 11:30, the moon was bright enough to inspire a male woodcock. His *"peent, peent"* calls were the first I heard this season. Also heard my first flicker yesterday.

March 24

The horned owls and screech owls are hooting tonight! I haven't heard the horned owls be so vocal in a couple of weeks. The screechers have been doing most of the calling. I wonder if the full (or almost so) moon has something to do with it.

March 30

Hepatica blooming today. I went out shortly after sunset to sneak up on the woodcock. On my way, I watched the big horned owl through binoculars as he left the willow from the northwest corner of the pond and dropped low over the area where the woodcock was. The owl paid little attention to the woodcock.

I, on the other hand, did watch the woodcock for quite some time. I got much closer to his "peenting" ground than the binoculars could focus.

It was quite therapeutic to watch him strut back and forth, pumping his head a bit as he called. He took off low on his display flights and I generally lost him behind bushes blocking my view. He was working hard for an unseen (to me) mate.

March 31

Another night of woodcock watching. Got out earlier tonight, before the birds started calling. I was looking down for woodcock hangouts instead of looking up. When I did look up at a familiar dead tree, I noticed that one of the branch stubs looked a bit different. Perhaps, it cracked in a strong wind.

I took a closer look just in time to notice that it was the great horned owl, perched and looking like part of the tree. In a silent second, the owl headed off for an elm across the pond. As he sat in plain view, the sun finished setting.

While walking back to the main trail, I heard the "peent, peent." Tonight, the woodcock was just a bit south from where I had found him the night before.

In an effort to blend in, I chose dark corduroys and a sweatshirt to wear. Looking at my white tennis shoes and socks, I realized I hadn't really thought it through.

I moved carefully, but not too quietly, in an effort to get closer to the woodcock. My white shoes and the crunching leaves did not distract him from his mating show.

He took short steps (maybe long strides to a woodcock) and suddenly pulled up short. Then, he started off in another, seemingly at random, direction.

His actions were reminiscent of a toy robot I had as a kid. When confronted with a wall or other obstacle, the robot turned and proceeded in a different direction. The woodcock moved as if he was hitting invisible obstacles.

Every now and then the bird would make a longer than average run, maybe eight to ten feet, and then turn and start again. He would often take wing after one of these longer rushes.

He started north, curved to the east over the pond and out of my line of sight. As he was whistling and twittering overhead, I moved closer to where I thought the woodcock would land.

When the bird stopped calling, I stopped moving. In sailed the woodcock from the lighted western sky. He had a bat-like quality as he turned his wings flaps down and the sun shown through his brown translucent feathers.

April 3

Estimating distance at night is a funny thing. Judging by the sounds, I was very close to the woodcock this evening. Right before each call, I could hear a brief water-drop sound. I cupped by ears to focus on this subtle whoop/whistle just before each "*peent.*"

It was as if he was clearing his beak or made the noise as he breathed in just prior to making the much louder "*peent.*" I was listening so intently that the woodcock's take-off startled me.

Once again, I adjusted my position in hopes of an even closer viewing or, should I say, listening. By this time, stars were visible overhead and the ground was quite dark.

I spot him low in the western sky as he returns in near silence. He lands so close that I can hear his feet hit the ground. Perhaps, I am too close as I can hear him walk quickly away.

The woodcock's calls diminish in intensity and regularity. I am suddenly aware of a variety of itches that, just minutes ago, wouldn't have dared present themselves.

Minutes pass. Darkness has completely enveloped the scene. I wonder where he went.

Slowly, I step towards home when I hear that characteristic whirring/whistle of the woodcock's wings. No nuptial display this time; just a sudden start to some secluded spot.

At sunrise, the dance begins anew.

ROBIN ROUNDUP

The next time somebody tells me they just saw the "first robin of spring." I'll be tempted to respond, "How do you know it isn't the last robin of winter?" You see, while many robins do migrate, many others have been here all winter long. Robins as spring harbingers? It's just another nature myth.

To be precise, I'm talking about the American robin which is not to be confused with the European robin which it was when English settlers first saw our robin and named it after their robin. Confused yet? O.K., the robin redbreast of Europe has, as the name suggests, a red chest. So early settlers, not known for their ornithological expertise, called every bird with a red breast a robin. The bluebird was a blue robin, the rufous-sided towhee was the ground robin, and the red-breasted merganser (a duck) was the sea robin.

Nowadays, the term robin applies to the one we've all seen pulling worms from our lawns. Speaking of worms, you might be wondering, what do the wintering robins eat? Berries, berries, and more berries. They will eat a wide variety of fruits including hackberry, cherry, juniper, dogwood, sumac, mulberry, and hawthorn. Research in New Jersey showed that wintering robins fed on larger fruits more efficiently than smaller fruits. By doing so, they were able consume more while swallowing fewer fruits in shorter visits.

Their taste for dark purple pokeberries saved robins from being served on our dining room tables. Hungry colonists discovered that robins were a tasty delicacy and large numbers were shot and trapped until the mid-1800s.

Not surprisingly, bird lovers objected to this practice but their protests fell on deaf ears. In the mid-nineteenth century, newspaper accounts observed that robins eat copious amounts of juicy pokeberries, a poisonous fruit. The reports included exaggerated claims that several persons had died from dining on robins that had eaten pokeberries. As you might expect, the demand for robin meat ceased almost instantly.

Robins & DDT

As mentioned earlier, a robin's diet includes earthworms. This aspect of their diet led to dramatic robin die-offs first studied on the campus of **Michigan State** University in the mid-1950s. It was in this decade that the use of the insecticide DDT gained in popularity.

As chronicled in her 1962 classic, *Silent Spring*, Rachel Carson reported that spraying DDT for Dutch elm disease began at MSU in 1954. The following year, the adjoining city of East Lansing joined in. It wasn't long before it became evident that robins on the 185-acre campus were dying of insecticide poisoning. At the time, proponents of DDT claimed that it was "harmless to birds."

How did DDT get into the robins? Credit goes to Dr. Roy Barker of the Illinois Natural History Survey for answering this question. His work, published in 1958, showed that DDT clung to the leaves of trees and did not wash away in the rain. Keep in mind that in areas where elms were thick, the amount of DDT sprayed could total as much as 23 pounds per acre!

In the autumn the leaves fell to the ground and, with the help of earthworms, began to decompose and return to the soil. It turns out earthworms are resistant to DDT. DDT residues in worms can reach up to five times the levels in the surrounding soils.

The following spring, when the worms were once again accessible, the trouble for robins really began. As few as eleven earthworms could carry enough DDT to kill a robin. A robin could easily eat that many worms in fifteen minutes. As you can imagine, the results of spraying DDT had a devastating impact on the robin population at MSU. In 1954, the campus population of robins was estimated to be 370. By the time *Silent Spring* was published, approximately two dozen robins remained at MSU. By 1973, thanks to Rachel Carson and scientific research, most uses of DDT were banned in the United States.

Folklore Revisited

Interestingly, the DDT story puts a modern spin on an old British superstition about robins. In Devon, a local saying warned: "Kill a robin or a wren— never prosper, boy or man." In East Lansing and elsewhere in this country where injudiciously applied pesticides killed many a robin, this saying rings true.

THE LEGENDARY PARAKEETS
OF CHICAGO'S HYDE PARK

How is it that a South American parakeet had an African-American champion when it came to nest in a North American city? The story involves immigration, legal action, public relations, and political connections. The bird is the monk parakeet, the champion was the late Harold Washington, and the city is Chicago.

Monk parakeets, at about a foot in length, are noticeably larger than your average pet store parakeets. As you can see from the inside back cover, without its lengthy tail the bird would only be half as long. Overall, the monk parakeet is green in color with an olive-yellow band across its upper abdomen, and a gray face and chest. This gray hood, or cowl, was reminiscent of religious attire; hence, the sobriquet "monk."

Accidental & Intentional Releases

In an article in the December, 1973 *Wilson Bulletin,* John Bull of the American Museum of Natural History describes the parakeet's arrival in the New York area:

> *Multiple releases by design and by accident have resulted in a sizeable resident population in southeastern New York, and the adjacent portions of Connecticut and New Jersey. These releases, that is escaped birds, came from broken crates at Kennedy Airport, accidental escapes from pet shops, aviaries, and private owners, as well as intentional releases by persons tired of caring for these parrots.*

By 1973, parakeet sightings were also reported from Ohio, Indiana, Texas, and California. That same year in Asheville, North Carolina, a large flock of breeding parakeets was reported. Bull's account of the New York population of parakeets applies to other regions of the country as well. These random parakeet colonies were the result of either accidental or purposeful release by pet stores, zoos, or individuals. For example, in Asheville where the large flock was seen, escaped pet parakeets have been observed since the early 1960s.

The species originally ranged from southern Brazil and central Bolivia through Uruguay and Paraguay to south-central Argentina. While the northern part of this range is considered subtropical, the southern part is a temperate zone with weather conditions not unlike those experienced in Washington D.C., Indianapolis, or San Francisco. Further, monk parakeets can be found living in the foothills of the Andes Mountains at elevations as high as 3000 feet. At this height, temperatures can drop to twenty degrees Fahrenheit. This ability to exist in a temperate climate sets the monk parakeet, or "loro" as it is called in Argentina, apart from most other members of the parrot clan.

Another notable characteristic of this South American immigrant is its gregarious nature. Be it Chicago, Illinois or Rosario, Argentina, monk parakeets are almost always spotted in groups. Unlike any other species of parrot, pairs of monks nest together in large stacks of sticks that resemble, as one observer described a Chicago nest, "a miniature haystack that had been flung into the green ash tree by some capricious tornado." These colonial nests can weigh up to several hundred pounds and be as large as twenty cubic feet in size, although smaller nests are more common. In South America they prefer to build these nests in thorny trees. If appropriate trees aren't available, they will build their nests in man-made structures such as utility poles, church steeples, radio towers, and in the broken glass globes of decorative sidewalk lights.

A shared nest structure does not mean one big pile of eggs. Instead, within the haystack of sticks can be found as many as a dozen individual compartments, each being used by a breeding pair of birds. Each chamber is approximately seven inches in diameter and fifteen inches deep. The adults lay a clutch of five to nine eggs once a year.

Many of our native birds have little to do with their own nests after the breeding season. The monks, on the other hand, use their imposing stick edifice year-round. This is obviously useful when withstanding either North or South America's winters. When it gets extremely cold they use other edifices, such as fire escapes on the lee side of tall apartment buildings, to protect them from the wind. Thanks to such strategies, Chicago's resident monk parakeets are able to withstand cold spells when the temperatures fall well below zero.

Of course, Chicago's parakeets, which live in the Hyde Park neighborhood not far from the University of Chicago, had generous benefactors in the form of human neighbors. More than one Hyde Park family maintained feeding stations in their backyards and were delighted to have the parakeets stop by for a free meal. These meals can make a critical difference on extremely frigid days.

Due to dietary habits in their homeland, which can include fruit crops, the Argentine and Uruguayan governments have tried to reduce parakeet numbers by poisoning, netting, burning, and shooting. The birds have even had a bounty placed on their heads. None of the above efforts, however, had a significant impact on the parakeet population.

Chicago's Parrot Troopers

On this continent, many, but not all, government bodies have reacted negatively to the arrival of these Neotropical immigrants. In Chicago, the birds actually had what some Chicago reporters call "clout." In 1983, Chicago elected its first African-American mayor, the late Harold Washington.

Mayor Washington's apartment building had a direct view of one of the largest parakeet nests in the country. Their presence was not lost on the Mayor who said: "We are all pleased and grateful that these fine parrots have chosen to settle in the great city of Chicago. I think of them as an omen signifying better times ahead for the entire community. For me personally, they have been a good-luck talisman."

An argument could be had over how much luck the birds brought the mayor. On the other hand, the fact that the mayor was a good-luck talisman for the parakeets cannot be challenged. As a high-profile politician, the mayor required around-the-clock police protection. This meant that at any time, day or night, a police car was parked directly in front of the mayor's residence which, fortuitously, was directly below the monks' nest. Needless to say, nobody messed with the Mayor's nest(s).

As fate would have it, Mayor Washington died shortly after being re-elected in November of 1987. Not long thereafter, the Hyde Park

WANTED

Be on the lookout for this ALIEN bird that is attempting to establish itself in the United States.

NAME: Monk parakeet (<u>Myiopsitta monachus</u>) alias Quaker parakeet alias gray-headed parakeet.

DESCRIPTION: A dove-sized parakeet, greenish-gray back with lemon-yellow belly. Forecrown, cheeks, forethroat, and breast are light gray with darker feather edges. Wing feathers are blue-gray with a long pointed bluish-green tail. The feet are dark colored and both sexes are alike in coloration.

KNOWN RESIDENCES: Lives in a bulky communal nest made of sticks; has already been reported from many States.

LIVELIHOOD: Exotic pet inside homes, but reverts to agricultural pest when in the wild.

VIOLATIONS: Has large appetite for corn, fruit, grain and other seeds. Travels in large flocks to raid agricultural fields and orchards.

Information is needed on the distribution and number of monk parakeets in your area. If you see this bird please contact:

> U. S. FISH & WILDLIFE SERVICE
> 10600 HIGGINS RD. - ROOM 204
> ROSEMONT, ILLINOIS 60018

Bureau of Sport Fisheries and Wildlife
Federal Building Fort Snelling
Twin Cities, Minnesota 55111 4/24/73

In 1973, the U.S. Fish and Wildlife Service put out this wanted poster for the "alien" parakeet.

parakeets' luck began to take a turn for the worse. In the spring of 1988, the United States Department of Agriculture Animal Damage Control (ADC) Office announced plans to remove the birds from Hyde Park.

The neighborhood's parakeet admirers were not about to stand by and watch the feds swoop down on their birds. Attorney Robert Stone, a Hyde Park resident, organized the Harold Washington Memorial Parrot Defense Fund. In one newspaper account, Douglas Anderson, then President of the Chicago Audubon Society, pointed out that Chicago now had "the largest nesting place of monk parakeets in North America." Somehow, this all seemed fitting, that the largest nest should be in the city with the tallest building.

Many of the arguments made in support of Chicago's parakeets are very appropriate to this multi-cultural city. As one "parrot trooper" put it, "To find we have an aesthetic element right here in Chicago from South America, it was a natural direction for me." Robert Stone adds, "Whenever a professor comes in from Europe and I give him a tour of Chicago, I drive by and point out the parrots." Another observer succinctly commented, "We are a nation of immigrants, and so are they." The ruckus caused by Hyde Park's parakeet defenders successfully postponed the parakeets' removal.

OK, I can hear the critics thinking, "the immigration stuff is nice but what about the agricultural threat?" One has to consider these threats on a case by case basis. Hyde Park, for example, is a long way from an apple orchard or grape vineyard. Frankly, that colony of parakeets poses little or no agricultural threat.

Some ADC officials have argued that the monk parakeet could be the next starling. Given the decades that have passed since breeding colonies have been observed in various states, the evidence suggests that breeding parakeets will never be anything other than a scattered and local phenomena. If they were going to spread like starlings, they would have. Also, given their colonial nesting habits, removing parakeets is an easy matter. Even if I'm wrong and monks become widespread, I would still question control efforts.

Illinois' Native Parrots

Let me tell you about another parakeet that lived in North America. Like the monk parakeet, it was about a foot long and mostly green in color. Like the monk parakeet, it was from the New World, travelled in flocks, and liked to eat fruit and seeds. Like the monk parakeet, it was kept as a caged bird by some and shot at by others, especially farmers. Like Hyde Park's monks, this parakeet was so associated with the Land of Lincoln that it was often referred to as the "Illinois Parrot." I am, of course, referring to the Carolina parakeet.

Along with the Great Auk, Labrador Duck, and Passenger Pigeon, the Carolina parakeet was one of the first species to be pushed off this continent into extinction by the expansion of European settlers. The thing that amazes me is that we were able to extirpate these species with such primitive technology. Think about it; pesticides, bulldozers, and chainsaws had yet to be invented. We eradicated the Carolina parakeet the old-fashioned way; we shot it.

Why such wholesale gunning of a species? People of that era

took up arms against the parakeets for a variety of reasons, but the most common shooters were landowners who objected to the birds feeding on their fruits and grains.

The stories of parakeet shootings couldn't be more poignant. Surviving birds had an unusual habit of returning to the scene, as if to mourn their dead, making them easy targets as well. This behavior was described by Audubon who wrote:

> ...the husbandman approaches them with perfect ease, and commits great slaughter among them. All the survivors rise, shriek, fly around about for a few minutes, and again alight on the very place of most imminent danger. The gun is kept at work; eight or ten, or even twenty, are killed at every discharge. The living birds, as if conscious of the death of their companions, sweep over their bodies, screaming as loud as ever, but still return to the stack to be shot at ....

The wholesale slaughter of Carolina parakeets was protested by ornithologists. In 1889, writing about the Illinois parrot, Robert Ridgway stated in *Birds of Illinois* that:

> The avian fauna of Illinois has lost no finer or more interesting member than the present species, which is probably now everywhere extinct within our borders, though fifty years ago it was of more or less common occurrence throughout the State.

The story of Illinois' two parakeets raises two interesting questions. First, could the monk parakeet be filling a niche left by the passing of the Carolina parakeet? That is a question best debated by taxonomists and other specialists.

I believe, however, that the second question is the more relevant. Unlike the niche argument, this question is more likely to be fodder for ethicists than for scientists. What does our reaction to these two parakeets tell us about our culture's relationship with nature?

Parakeet Legacies

The last Carolina parakeet, housed at the Cincinnati Zoo, died in 1914. In the 100+ years since that parakeet's death, our culture has become aware of air pollution, water pollution, overpopulation, habitat loss, and endangered species. Hopefully, we know that we share the earth with an incredible wealth of diverse species and habitats. The planet and its occupants are not here merely to serve us.

Yet the arguments offered by many wildlife officials for the removal of the monk parakeets (the birds are agricultural pests) are the very same ones that our predecessors used to extirpate the Carolina parakeet. It appears that we cannot tolerate a species we perceive to be in our way, regardless if that species is exotic or endangered.

Recent developments in Chicago's parakeet story suggest that, thanks to the monks' uncanny talent for public relations, we have at least learned some tolerance. At the far end of Hyde Park, opposite from the existing colony of monk parakeets, sits the DuSable Museum of African-American History. The museum's curator is Ramon Price, the late Mayor Washington's half brother. In the spring of 1992, the museum was constructing a new addition. In a nearby tree, another construction project was underway. The arboreal builders were, of course, monk parakeets.

Why was their arrival at DuSable described as an act of fate? Because the museum addition, which opened in February, 1993, was dedicated as the Harold Washington wing. Price said the nearby parakeet nest was reminiscent of an African tradition in which it was customary to incorporate an "authorizing thing" from the old village in a new settlement.

Price also commented on how the birds have become an educational opportunity for school children who are lined up outside the museum. I tell them to look for the green parakeets, and the story of how they were Mayor Washington's birds."

The legend continues.

SHRIKES!

I like starting the New Year going for a walk. Here are a few reasons why you might want to join me:

1) As we all know, some people overindulge on New Year's Eve. Nothing clears the cobwebs from your brain quicker than a walk outside in the refrigerated January air.

2) As hard as this might be to believe, football is also an intoxicant that is best consumed in moderation. A long walk should get you out of at least one of the never-ending parade of bowl games.

3) Ignore reasons 1 & 2, here's the real reason. The football addicts will stay inside. The hung-over partiers will be groaning in bed… watching football. On Jan. 1, you are likely to have Mother Nature all to yourself or you will run in to people that enjoy being outside like you do. That's why we always have a New Year's Day walk at Stillman Nature Center.

On one particular New Year's Day walk, we were concentrating on birds. We saw many of the "usual suspects:" chickadees, mourning doves, crows, plus a great horned owl and a red-tailed hawk. The most exciting sighting was a northern shrike perched at the top of a slender tree.

Before getting to our shrike, let's take a look at the owl and the hawk. These fellows, along with other birds of prey, use their feet to grab, puncture, stun, and/or kill their prey. I say "and/or kill," because some might use their hooked beak for the final termination.

Songbirds, technically called passerines, use their beaks to capture bugs, worms, or berries. However, there is one group of songbirds that prey on vertebrate animals: the shrikes.

Butcher Birds

The scientific name for the shrike we saw, *Lanius exubitor*, says it all. Translated it reads, "butcher sentinel." Our New Year's bird was definitely acting like a watchman waiting for a mouse or bird to make a mistake.

The northern shrike, by the way, is about the size of a robin. It is gray above, white below, wears a black mask, and sports contrasting black-and-white patterns on its wings and tail. It is a winter resident in our area, often arriving by late October and heading back to Canada and Alaska in March.

Oh, you want to hear about the butcher part. Well, this medium-sized songbird will store meat, like a butcher, on hooks. Of course, its meat locker is the great outdoors and its hooks are forks in tree branches, thorns, or the barbs on barbed wire. That's right, it will stick a mouse or grasshopper on a thorn and come back to dine on it later. Other times, the thorn is simply used to secure the prey as it tears it apart. In effect, the thorns supplant the raptor talons this passerine is lacking.

Raptor Wannabe

That is not to say it doesn't have strong feet. As a licensed bird bander, I had the opportunity to hold one. Not surprisingly, I chose to wear gloves to protect my hand from both its bill and feet.

Like a songbird, the northern shrike catches small mammals, insects, and an occasional reptile by grabbing them with its beak. Some birds will be caught in its bill but most are captured with the feet.

Folklore recognizes this connection with the raptors. Northern shrikes can be found across northern Europe and Asia. There is a European legend that describes a race between a hawk and a shrike. Much as the tortoise beat the hare, the shrike, thanks to its persistence, beats the hawk.

The French word for the related red-backed shrike, *l'ecorcheur* or "flayer," brings me back to the butcher bird term.

Glass Houses

Not only does the northern shrike store its prey like a butcher but it prepares them like a butcher as well. I'll quote from a scientific account of the shrike at work. "Shrike typically pulls apart impaled vertebrates starting at head.... Begins by tearing at eyes or mouth and working skin and flesh loose toward neck." Is it any wonder that the Nunamiut people of Alaska call the northern shrike *irirgik*, the "eye extractor."

Disgusted by this gross description? Not me. I get a kick from these pint-sized predatory rascals. If you are bothered by the butcher bird's habits, stroll down the meat aisle of your local supermarket. Take a close look at the neatly packaged red slabs of meat. Those who live in glass houses...

SANDHILL CRANES FOR CRYING OUT LOUD

The ultimate value in these marshes is wildness, and the crane is wildness incarnate. But all conservation of wildness is self-defeating, for to cherish we must see… and when enough have seen, there is no wilderness left to cherish.

—Aldo Leopold (1949)

This quotation from Leopold's classic *Sand County Almanac* does not paint a pretty picture. He's basically saying that as wild marshes disappear so will sandhill cranes. Today, sandhill cranes are doing quite well. Before we get to their history with humans, let's review some of the basics.

The Brass Section

Sandhill cranes (*Grus canadensis*) are three to four feet tall with a very long neck and legs. They are generally gray in color with a red forehead.

Sometimes similarly-shaped great blue herons and great egrets are mistakenly called cranes. The egret is easy to separate from the crane thanks to its all white color.

The dark-colored great blue heron can be a bit more difficult to distinguish from a crane. When in flight, both egrets and herons fly with necks folded into a compressed 'S'. Cranes fly with their necks outstretched.

The other obvious characteristic that separates cranes from herons and egrets is their marvelous call. Herons and egrets are essentially hoarse squawkers.

One of the reasons Aldo Leopold wrote that "the crane is wildness incarnate" is no doubt because of their calls. Let's return to *Sand County Almanac* for this poetic description of the cranes' timeless vocalizations:

> *Now comes a baying of some sweet-throated hound, soon the clamor of a responding pack. Then a far clear blast of hunting horns, out of the sky into the fog.*

It is not so much the sweetness but the design of the throat that explains the crane's ability to trumpet and bugle. Their elongated trachea, a yard or more in length, coils around their breastbone. Think of it as the ornithological equivalent of a trombone slide.

When a flock of sandhills is migrating overhead, their haunting cries are often heard long before squinting eyes can make out the birds. Is it any wonder that the word "crane" has its origin in the Indo-European *kar* meaning "to cry out."

Craning My Neck

Cry out is exactly what I did one day while riding in a friend's car just a short distance from the nature center. I was looking out the window at a relatively new berm, the kind you see edging young subdivisions in our area.

I like to scan and see what kind of trees were planted, if they're being watered, and the like. As I was looking, damn if I didn't see a crane. I quickly urged my companion to turn around so I could make sure. Yep, there it was walking along a suburban berm as if that was what cranes do these days.

Now, I knew cranes have been nesting in the neighborhood, so to speak, but it was still a bit jarring to see one in this newly created landscape. Wasn't this crane contradicting Aldo Leopold?

Getting to the Crex of the Issue

During Leopold's life (1887–1948), the sandhill crane disappeared as a breeding bird from Illinois (1890), Iowa (1905), and Ohio (1926). The primary causes of the bird's decline was agricultural expansion, hunting, and drainage of wetlands.

Let's take a closer look at Wisconsin, where *Sand County Almanac* is set. This was also the state where I saw my first young sandhill while visiting Crex Meadows wildlife area in 1975.

This refuge is a combination of extensive sandy plains and large marshes. Beginning in the mid-nineteenth century, settlers attempted to farm this land. By 1890, large-scale drainage projects had drastically reduced the amount of wetlands.

In 1912, the Crex Carpet Company bought 23,000 acres and set up work "camps" to harvest the grasses in the area, The Company went bankrupt in 1933, but the "Crex" name remained.

Besides the grass rug makers, most of the farmers, and the cranes, now that I think of it, had abandoned the Crex area as well. During the 1930s, there were only about twenty-five breeding pairs of cranes to be found anywhere in Wisconsin.

In 1946, the State bought 12,000 acres of the old Crex land and within a year began constructing dikes to regulate the water flow in the area. Currently, there are over twenty miles of dikes along with a system of well-maintained roads, observation areas, and so on.

Such an intensely managed area does not seem to fit Leopold's vision of wilderness, yet the cranes have been nesting here for decades.

Crex Meadows serves as a model of what was happening

elsewhere during the twentieth century. Across the Midwest, many of the marginal farmlands were abandoned, wetlands were protected, and hunting was prohibited. As a result nesting cranes returned to Illinois (1979), Ohio (1987), and Iowa (1992).

The other reason I concentrated on the Dairy State is because the 1979 Illinois crane nest was just over the border from Wisconsin, This illustrates how the sandhills are expanding their range.

Interestingly, the cranes' nests are not limited to untamed marshes. Nowadays, their nests can be found in smaller wetlands and even hay meadows, and birds are regularly seen feeding in cornfields. Besides wild berries and insects, today's cranes are quite fond of wheat, barley, sorghum and corn, not exactly native rarities.

Not being too picky about where you nest and what you eat helps explain why sandhills are now the most abundant species of crane in the world. In fact, several states now allow sandhill cranes to be hunted.

Sandhills Updated

All of which brings me back to that suburban berm. The crane I saw was hardly an icon of "wildness incarnate." On the other hand, it was symbolic of a species that has survived by adapting to change.

By the way, this species earned its name because, during migration, many congregate along the Platte River near Nebraska's Sandhills. So I'm wondering, should we rename the suburban birds the *berm cranes*? How about the *burb cranes*?

I got it. S*odhill cranes*.

A FOOLISH WAG TALE

But I will find him when he lies asleep,
And in his ear I'll hollo "Mortimer!"
Nay, I'll have a starling shall be taught to speak
Nothing but "Mortimer," and give it him
To keep his anger still in motion.

—*Henry IV, Part One* William Shakespeare

This fateful quotation, taken from the quick-tempered Hotspur's invective against the king, led Eugene Schiefflin on a whimsical quest to acclimatize to the New World all the birds mentioned by the bard of Avon. Schiefflin released 120 starlings in New York in the early 1890s.

Truth be told, Schiefflin should just be credited with underwriting the first successful release of starlings in the U.S. It was actually William Bartels, a bird importer, who handled the release at Schiefflin's behest. The introduction of these birds to the New World was more successful than anyone could have imagined.

Starlings were viewed with a kinder eye in the Old World than in the New. This is evident from the roles they played in many works of art. With this in mind, perhaps it would be appropriate for us to take another look at this oft-maligned bird.

Shakespeare was right. European starlings, like Hill Mynas to which they are related, can be taught to speak. These birds' innate ability to mimic was first noted by the ancient Romans. The Roman poet Statius penned the following:

> *Let the learned birds be gathered together here,*
> *To which Nature gave a renowned right of speaking;*
> *Let the raven lament aloud, and the starling*
> *Inwardly remembering to send forth sounds ...*

Pliny, the great Roman natural historian, also described a "learned" starling, "Caesar's young men had a starling, also nightingales, trained in Greek and Latin conversation." I don't know about you, but for me, a former Latin student, Pliny's comment generates strange and wondrous visions.

Which one of Caesar's men do you suppose kept a talking bird? A front line centurion? No, probably not. A messenger or staff wine taster? Doubtful. How about one of his personal scribes? Now we're talking—I mean, the starling is talking.

So, what might the bird be saying? I can just see it... It is late in the evening and the midnight olive oil is burning. Caesar's poor intellectual slave is transcribing a rough copy of the emperor's now famous *Commentaries On The Gallic Wars* when his caged pet bursts out with, "Gallia-est-divisa-in-tres-partes-Gallia-est-divisa-in-tres-partes." To which the scribe's translated response would no doubt be, "Shut up, you damn bird."

Apparently, the custom of keeping a pet starling carried on

through the centuries and was not only captured in stories but on canvas. It was about 1528 when Hans Holbein, famous for his portrait of English statesman Sir Thomas More, painted *A Lady with A Pet Squirrel And A Starling.* The title doesn't mention that the bird is a pet, but I'm willing to bet it was. Of course, I'm not willing to bet as much as this painting recently sold for. In the spring of 1992, it was sold to the National Gallery in London for about $20 million. Not bad for a bird few people like to see in real life.

As you might imagine, I was curious about the identity of the woman with the pet starling. Art scholars suggest it is Thomas More's adopted daughter, Margaret Giggs. One can only wonder what this starling might have learned from his owner's adopted father, a man who coined the word "utopia" and was later beheaded for offending King Henry VIII.

As described earlier, Shakespeare mentioned a talking starling. Generally, classic English literature overlooks starlings—not because they were shunned but because they were not common birds during much of this literary era.

Elsewhere in Europe, however, the starling, once again in the hands of a misunderstood genius, was making an important cultural contribution. This time the medium was not poetry, plays, or painting; it was the piano.

In Austria, on May 27, 1784, a customer dashed into a local pet store. He was stupefied to hear a caged bird whistling the Allegretto theme from Mozart's G major piano concerto. He paid thirty-four Kreuzer for the bird and named him Vogel-Stahrl. This common bird soon became a cherished pet. The customer, on the other hand, was not your everyday passerby. His name—Wolfgang Amadeus Mozart.

We can be sure of the starling purchase because Mozart duly recorded the transaction and the date in his account book. The G major concerto is entered in his catalog of works on April 12 of the same year. How could Vogel-Stahrl possibly have learned Mozart's tune?

There are three possible explanations. Some scholars maintain that the concerto was based on the starling's whistles. If the dates on Mozart's records were reversed, that is, if he had purchased the bird before writing the concerto, then this would be a very attractive theory. Unfortunately, this is not the case. Perhaps Mozart fudged the entry date.

Mimicry researchers Meredith West and Andrew King offer an explanation that hinges on Mozart's shopping habits. They suggest that Mozart was a regular visitor to the pet store. As any contemporary mall patron can tell you, it is not uncommon to see pet lovers or just curious shoppers browse through a pet store without making a purchase. West and King's theory suggests that Mozart whistled the finale during one of his preliminary visits, later discovering that one of the store's caged birds had come to mimic it almost perfectly.

In those days, people who raised birds for sale often trained them to whistle distinct melodies. The thinking was that a particular tune might appeal to a potential customer. The training was done with the help of a flageolet, a simplified flutelike instrument. As any birder knows, starlings easily mimic whistles and whistle like calls.

If West and King's supposition is correct and Mozart was a regular visitor to the pet store, then the first theory also becomes plausible. West and King argue that Mozart whistled to the starling. I propose a different scenario. Imagine our eccentric, creative composer walking into a store that housed, say, at least a half-dozen caged birds, each whistling its individual melody. Could not Mozart, whether consciously or unconsciously, have picked up a tune that later reappeared in the G major piano concerto?

As much as I like that idea, I think a third explanation is most believable. Mozart-scholar Eric Blom writes that the G major piano concerto has a "folksong-like theme in the finale." Later he adds, "We find the same kind of Austrian folksong flavor in other things in G major." Just as Shakespeare borrowed plots for his plays from historical stories, a classical composer would borrow from folk songs. Popular folk tunes were commonly taught to young birds to make them more salable; thus, it was not an unlikely coincidence for Mozart and a starling to derive inspiration from the same popular Austrian folk song. The odds of Mozart hearing this starling, however, make for an interesting calculation.

Mozart's starling died June 4, 1787, just a few days after the death of Mozart's father, Leopold. Upon the bird's death, Wolfgang arranged a funeral procession, complete with veiled guests, for the starling's burial in the garden at his lodgings. Participants were encouraged to join in as he offered the following humorous requiem:

A little fool lies here
Whom I held dear—
A starling in the prime

Of his brief time,
Whose doom it was to drain
Death's bitter pain.
Thinking of this, my heart
Is riven apart.
Oh, reader! Shed a tear,
You also, here.
He was not naughty, quite,
But gay and bright,
And under all his brag
A foolish wag.
This no one can gainsay
And I will lay
That he is now on high,
and from the sky,
Praises me without pay
In his friendly way.
Yet unaware that death
has choked his breath,
And thoughtless of the one
Whose rime is thus well done.

Mozart's description of his pet as a friendly troublemaker is a sentiment shared by a well-known twentieth-century storyteller. P.L. Travers chose to include a mischievous talking starling in her charming Mary Poppins series.

The starling is able to talk with Mary Poppins as well as with a newborn child named Annabel. After learning the child's name, the starling exclaims, "That's a nice name! I had an Aunt Annabel. Used to live in Admiral Boom's chimney and died, poor thing, of eating green apples and grapes. I warned her, I warned her! But she wouldn't believe me!"

Later, the bird returns to babysit and, with luck, to make off with some Arrowroot biscuit.

"I'll keep watch," he said, in a whisper. "You go down and get a cup of tea." Mary Poppins stood up. "Mind you don't wake her, then!" The Starling laughed pityingly. "My dear girl, I have in my time brought up at least twenty broods of fledglings. I don't need to be told how to look after a mere baby." "Humph!" Mary Poppins walked to the cupboard and very pointedly put the biscuit tin under her arm before she went out and shut the door.

These stories of Mozart's "foolish wag" and Travers' mischief-making starling always bring a smile to my face. You see, I had a talking starling. His name was Rod—Rod starling. Now, I wouldn't want to suggest that Rod's caregiver was just another link in the chain of eccentric-genius starling owners, but I will argue that Rod was a likely representative of how today's generations of starlings interact with modern culture.

Rod's skill at mimicry was a testimonial to his myna heritage. More than once I dashed out of the shower to answer a ringing phone that turned out to be Rod. Of course, he was only as good as that which he heard. After Rod perfected his phone etiquette, "Hello, this is Mark Spreyer," he started saying something that sounded like, "He's a sick Jew."

Now, he didn't learn that from me. A visiting friend, who heard Rod for the first time, identified the phrase as, "Pleased to meet you." That translation made perfect sense. You see, I'm a Rolling Stones fan and Rod often heard *Sympathy for the Devil*, which repeats the phrase "pleased to meet you" throughout the song. Proper enunciation has never been a hallmark of rock singers, and Rod mimicked that lack of enunciation perfectly.

Just as Rod had not forgotten rock music, rock music has not forgotten starlings. One song that is regularly heard on today's classic rock stations is Cream's 1968 hit *White Room*. The opening lines are: "In a white room with black curtains near the station/ Black-roof country, no gold pavement, tired starlings."

As much as I like this song, I have to take exception to the phrase "tired starlings." Starlings are feathered bundles of nonstop energy. Like "jumbo shrimp," "tired starlings" is a classic oxymoron.

On the other hand, the lyrics do place starlings in an aging urban center, a setting many of us associate with the species.

It is interesting to reflect on how artists have depicted starlings over the centuries. The Romans, like Mozart, enjoyed them as caged birds. Mary Poppins' starling was both an urban dweller and a fruit raider. Rock music describes them as urban vagrants. Does this reflect a shift in starling activity or human activity?

Their survival in our altered landscapes has caused some people to recommend their slaughter. This brings me back to Caesar's learned starling. I wonder if it ever learned Caesar's famous words, "*Veni, vidi, vici,*" describing his decisive victory at the Battle of Zeta. Translated, these Latin words read, "I came, I saw, I conquered." When it comes to starlings in North America, no truer words were ever mimicked.

RAPTORS

Barred owl. Photo by Kristi Overgaard.

V. BIRDS OF PREY

Hawks and owls both have sharp talons and strong hooked beaks but they differ in their hunting tactics—one could almost say they differ in their approach to life. Hawks often miss their quarry; owls seldom miss. They are more apt to wait and wait until they are sure of making a kill.

—Frances Hamerstrom

FALCON PEREGRINATIONS

Just a short walk from your car, should you come for a Sunday visit to Stillman Nature Center, sits a peregrine falcon. It perches in a cage overlooking our lake. Even behind the screen, it takes command of the situation.

Unfortunately, this bird was found illegally shot in Lincolnwood and is permanently injured. Forty years ago, more or less, there weren't any resident peregrines to either admire or shoot at. At that time, the peregrine was still a federally endangered species.

This species' recovery is one I take personal pride in since I organized and directed Chicago's peregrine falcon release program during the 1980s. In Illinois, the spring of 1988 was an eventful time for these rare birds.

That year, I celebrated Mother's Day watching a peregrine falcon mother feeding her two chicks atop a Chicago office building. These were the first two peregrines hatched anywhere in Illinois in 37 years. So in the bird world, it was an auspicious Mother's Day indeed.

Decline Due to DDT

Peregrines were absent for nearly four decades thanks to DDT, a long-lasting insecticide that profoundly affects the reproductive metabolism of many bird species, notably birds of prey. In the case of the peregrine, the pesticide interferes with calcium absorption, resulting in egg shells so thin that they broke under the weight of the incubating parent.

By 1970, only 39 breeding pairs could be found in the continental United States— all west of the Mississippi. In 1973, DDT was banned from use in this country but, because of DDT's low solubility in water and its slow rate of chemical breakdown, the effects of the ban were not immediately realized.

At about the same time DDT was banned, the peregrine became a charter member of the federal government's newly established list of endangered species. The equally new Peregrine Fund, meanwhile, was successfully breeding peregrines in captivity. By 1975, the Peregrine Fund began releasing falcons at various sites including East Coast cities.

Cities may strike one as odd places to release endangered birds, but peregrines see nothing odd about taking up residence on structures built and occupied by humans. In an 1877 magazine article, George Boudin described a peregrine encounter:

> *On the 13th of September, 1868, I shot a fine specimen (male) at the corner of Fifth and Girard Avenue, Philadelphia. For nearly three weeks this bird of prey had made its home in St. Peter's steeple.*

Other remarkable examples of urban falcons were to be seen in the 1940s and '50s on New York's Regis Hotel and, most dramatically, on Montreal's Sun Life Assurance building where, over a period of 16 years, a female peregrine and three successive males raised a total of 21 young.

Sweet Home, Chicago

In 1986, atop another man-made structure— University Hall on the University of Illinois Chicago campus— a falcon release program was initiated by combining the talents of the Chicago Academy of Sciences, Illinois Department of Conservation, Lincoln Park Zoo, and the Chicago Audubon Society. It was my privilege to head this cooperative effort.

A male peregrine from the 1986 release was the father of the

two chicks I was watching on Mother's Day. The mother was released from Minneapolis in 1985. Such long-distance relationships are not unusual for these falcons hence the name peregrine, as in "peregrination."

In 1987, we released falcons from the water tower at Fort Sheridan. By 1988, a male from the tower mated with a female released from Rochester, Minnesota. Where was their nest? On a building in Milwaukee. See what I mean about peregrination?

No Longer Endangered

As mentioned earlier, peregrines were being released at a variety of locations and, in 1980, the first successful breeding of released falcons occurred in New Jersey. Between 1985 and 1988, pairs of peregrines could be found in, at least, 24 cities and towns. Of these,

21 pairs raised about 45 fledglings. Interestingly, nine of these urban locations had never hosted a peregrine release.

Studies done on the New Jersey falcon eggs found DDT present in high levels showing that birds continue to be exposed to contaminants.

By 1993, more than 100 peregrine nests were found east of the Mississippi River and in 1999, the U.S. Fish and Wildlife Service removed the peregrine falcon from the Endangered Species List. Approximately 1,600 pairs were breeding across the U.S. and Canada.

Personally Speaking

Over the years, I have seen peregrines everywhere from a cliff in South Africa to Minnesota's rocky Lake Superior shoreline. While these locations are more picturesque than downtown Chicago, no peregrine sighting will hold as much meaning or joy for me than watching the newly hatched chicks at the corner of Adams and Wacker.

WINTER'S OWL

The January full moon is often described as the owl moon. This is because great horned owl courtship is in full swing during the first month of the year. Courting owls are rarely seen, but here at Stillman, they are often heard: *Hoo/hoo - hoo, Hoo ... Hoo - hoo/hoo - hoo.*

That deep, low call means trouble for cottontails, squirrels, chipmunks, rats, mice, skunks, pigeons, sparrows, crows, crayfish, snakes and anything else that breathes and looks edible to a great horned owl.

The important thing to remember is that great horned owls are opportunists, not specialists like some other owls. What they choose off the menu is determined by its availability. If the rabbit population is high, they'll eat rabbits. If the mouse population soars, they'll eat mice. I'm not talking about one or two mice. In one night, a horned owl will hunt as many mice as half a dozen cats.

This is not to suggest that a great horned owl is six times larger than a cat, although it may seem that big if you're surprised by one flying overhead at dusk. A male owl rarely reaches three pounds and the female averages between three-and-a-half and four pounds. They range in length from eighteen inches to two feet and have a wingspan in the neighborhood of four-and-a-half feet. The owl's colors are a mixture of brown, buff and black. This mix easily camouflages the bird during the day.

At night, such subtle tones are difficult to distinguish. Instead, the observer should look for two "horns" or tufts of feathers on either side of the head. Good binoculars will help you spot the bird's other identifying features that include large yellow eyes and a white patch of feathers on the throat (see cover photo).

Some of you may be wondering, "Just where does a bird this large nest?" The answer is, "Anywhere it wants to." And "anywhere" includes right here at the nature center.

Like other owls, the great horned owl does not build a nest. Instead, it simply "recycles" some other bird's nest. Being adaptable creatures, owls are not too particular about whose nest they use. It might be the old nest of a crow, squirrel, red-tailed hawk, great blue heron, or, as happened here at the nature center, a laundry basket filled with sticks and chips.

Since the owls nest in the dead of winter, most of these sites are "empty nesters." By the end of February, the owls have mated and are watching over a pair of eggs.

The variety of nest sites not only illustrates adaptability but also reflects the variety of habitats that can support a pair of horned owls. Take a look at the range map in a field guide to birds and you'll discover that the great horned owl is a year-round resident from the tree line in northern Canada and Alaska south throughout North, Central and South America.

So, why nest so early? By spring, when young owls are partially grown and especially ravenous, many other mammals are tending to their young families. Each animal family is just another fast food franchise to the owlets' parents. Also, as suggested earlier, it makes it easier to preempt a nest from its builder.

Does anyone mess with the young owl family? Not hardly. As Craighead and Craighead wrote in *Hawks, Owls and Wildlife,*

> *...the Horned owl is the most powerful bird, .. .it has preference as to its nest location and cannot be evicted by other raptors. It also can hunt or defend itself equally well by day or night. This is not true of the large hawks that might possibly dispute the owl's dominance...*

Should you hear the hooting of a great Homed owl this winter, take the time to venture into the night and see if you can find the bird making the call. You may not spot the owl but, whooo knows, you just might. As the child in Jane Yolen's classic book, *Owl Moon,* says:

> *When you go owling*
> *you don't need words*
> *or warm*
> *or anything but hope.*
> *That's what Pa says.*
> *The kind of hope that flies*
> *on silent wings*
> *under a shining*
> *Owl Moon.*

RED-SHOULDERED HAWKS

I sit in the top of my wood, my eyes closed.
Inaction, no falsifying dream
Between my hooked head and hooked feet:
Or in sleep rehearse perfect kills and eat.

The convenience of the high trees!
The air's buoyancy and the sun's ray
Are of advantage to me;
And the earth's face upward for my inspection.

—from *Hawk Roosting* by Ted Hughes

A few years ago, Stillman added a red-shouldered hawk (*Buteo lineatus*) to its collection of permanently injured raptors. The bird's imposing stare brought Hughes' poem to mind (see inside front cover). It also reminded me of how excited I was when I discovered a nest of red-shouldereds just a few miles from the nature center.

The Answer Kee

It was 1983; I was renting a house that was for sale and often asked to vacate the premises when the property was being shown. Perhaps it wasn't me they wanted out so much as it was Mountain, my 140-pound Alaskan malamute.

Anyway, I discovered that the local riding club maintained around sixty miles of trails that crisscrossed the area on both public and private properties. In retrospect, I imagine some Riding Club members might have taken a dim view of encountering me and Mountain plodding through their horses' droppings. But at the time,

I was just delighted to find trails that wound their way through woods and, in my neighborhood, near a small lake and stream.

It was there, in the spring, that I first heard the distinctive *kee-aah* call of a territorial red-shouldered hawk. Unlike the red-tailed hawk (*Buteo jamaicensis*), the red-shouldered hawk repeats its call several times and the drawn-out second syllable ends with a downward inflection. If you hear such a call be careful not to jump to conclusions. Blue jays can mimic this call to near perfection.

Buteo Review

As the scientific names indicate, red-tailed and red-shouldered hawks belong to the genus *Buteo*. Buteos can be told by their expansive wings and fan-shaped tail.

Red-tails are a very adaptable species that hunt rabbits and mice in open habitats. The omnipresent red-tail perched by the roadside lead many to think that all buteos are open-country hunters, leaving the forests to the accipiters.

Accipiters include the sharp-shinned (*Accipiter striatus*) and Cooper's hawks (*Accipiter cooperii*) which you might see hunting the birds at your backyard feeder. In contrast to buteos, accipiters have short, rounded wings and a long, rudder-like tail. The accipiters' body design facilitates adept aerial maneuvers required by their avian prey and wooded habitat.

As you probably know, it is never that simple in nature. Not all buteos are found in open spaces. In fact, red-shouldered hawks are forest dwelling buteos.

Going in the Red

Given its preference for forests, it is not surprising that the red-shouldered hawk has some accipiter qualities. Compared to other buteos, for example, it has a longer tail and more rounded wing-tips. Also, its flight action often involves fast, accipiter-like flapping.

When I spotted the hawk making the call along the horse trail, it was not the wing-tips I noticed. What caught my eye, as the bird sailed overhead, was the robin-red chest, the black tail with narrow white bands, and the "windows" (crescent-shaped translucent patches) located just inside each of the wing-tips.

Now that I've had a chance to work with a red-shouldered up close and personal, I have to say that I don't think there is a better looking hawk anywhere in Illinois.

Of course, red-shouldered hawks can be found outside of the Land of Lincoln. In fact there are four subspecies of red-shouldered hawks that range from Maine to Florida, west to east Texas and north to central Minnesota. A fifth isolated subspecies can be found along the Pacific Coast from southern Oregon down to Baja.

Your Neck of the Woods

Not only do the subspecies, as you might expect, vary in color but also in their tolerance of habitat alteration.

Encroaching civilization has not deterred the California subspecies. It can be seen from freeways nesting in exotic trees like eucalyptus. Elsewhere in the country, this has not been so.

During most of the last two centuries, red-shouldered hawks

apparently diminished from the eastern U.S. due to extensive logging. When I found that nest in 1983, it was on our state's endangered species list. The good news is that twenty years later, it was taken off the list. Luckily, once-farmed lands are reverting to forest.

However, a cautionary note is still in order. Even if a forest is merely thinned, it will no longer be attractive to a red-shouldered hawk. The less particular and more common red-tailed hawk will move in. Red-shouldered hawks prefer large tracts of woodland where, for the most part, the crowns of adjacent trees touch one another.

In this millennium, I have enjoyed visiting a nest of red-shouldered hawks located on private property in a nearby community. It reminded me of that first nest I found so many years ago.

At the time, I called the state to see what could be done to protect this endangered species but, since the property was in private hands, there was little they could do. Fortunately for those hawks, the homeowner liked the woods and the seclusion offered by the spacious nearby properties.

This was an early lesson for me in recognizing that valuable wildlife habitat is often found outside of county forest preserves and state parks.

With this in mind, I have a small request. Should you be fortunate enough to own property that includes riparian (aka stream bank) habitat, remember the red-shouldered hawk especially if you are considering removing some trees. If the trees remain, you will not only be providing a possible nest site for the hawks but also protecting ideal habitat for shade-loving wildflowers such as trout lily, white trillium, and toothwort.

Convenience of the High Trees

All of this brings me back for the next two stanzas of Ted Hughes' marvelous hawk poem.

My feet are locked upon the rough bark.
It took the whole of Creation
To produce my foot, my each feather:
Now I hold Creation in my foot

Or fly up, and revolve all slowly—
I kill where I please because it is all mine.
There is no sophistry in my body:
My manners are tearing off heads—

WHO HOOTS FOR YOU?

Imagine you've settled in your tent for the night at a tranquil forest campsite. As you are about to fall asleep, you are startled awake by a loud bird strenuously calling *"hoo-hoo-to-hoo-oo, hoo-hoo-hoo-to-whoooah"* Should you be lucky enough to have that experience, tip your hat to the barred owl, the classic hoot-owl (see photo on page 118).

In case you're wondering, I'm writing about barred owls because we recently added one to the nature center's educational collection of permanently injured raptors.

Owl as a Second Language
Contrary to popular opinion, many owls don't hoot. While great horned and barred owls do hoot, others screech, chatter, bark, wail, whoop, whinny, trill, howl and caterwaul.

That said, when it comes to A-No. 1, top-of-the-line hooting, you can't beat a barred owl. I should know, you see, because I'm bilingual. Yes, I can speak owl as well as human. So, if I may, here's a brief lesson on how to speak barred owl.

We'll start with the two-phrase hoot described above. Both sexes make this call which is used as a territorial advertisement. This hooting pattern is commonly phoneticized as, *"Who cooks for you? Who cooks for you-all?"*

Speaking of phonetics, to properly speak owl you'll need to work on the correct pronunciation. The first two syllables of the initial phrase and the first three of the latter are clear, deliberate, and low-toned. The last two hoots run together, with a strong accent on the penultimate one. O.K., are you practicing? Once you've got the two-phrase hoot down, it's time to study the caterwaul.

The caterwaul is performed by a dueting pair of owls and can last up to two minutes. It is composed of a raucous mix of cackles, whoops, caws, laughs, hoots, and gurgles. I clearly remember when I first heard this spine-chilling call. It sounded like a lunatic woman being run over by a truck.

March Madness

March is the month you are most likely to hear a barred owl duet. As noted Wisconsin ornithologist Frances Hamerstrom wrote, "March is the month of madness for barred owls; the breeding season is upon them, and instead of remaining shyly in the deep woods, they take to the open country…"

While barred owls are uncommon in our immediate area, they can be found in floodplain forests that edge many of our state's larger rivers. (See *Barred Owl Basics* on following pages.)

As you'll recall, Stillman has another raptor that is found in lowland forests, the red-shouldered hawk. So, how do they work this shared habitat?

Night and Day Shifts

Being nocturnal, the barred owl often roosts in trees and cavities or other secluded spots during the day. By the way, animals that are active during the day, like the red-shouldered hawk, are called *diurnal*.

If a habitat hosts an abundance of prey, it will have openings for both nocturnal and diurnal raptors. In this case, the similarly-sized red-shouldered hawk hunts mice and frogs during the day that the barred owl hunts at night. Other examples of this sunrise/sunset job switch include:

Day	*Night*
American Kestrel	E. Screech-owl
Northern Harrier	Short-eared Owl
Broad-winged Hawk	Long-eared Owl
Red-tailed Hawk	Great Horned Owl

Just because they work different shifts doesn't mean these raptor counterparts always get along. Great horned owls, for example, have been known to forcibly evict red-tails from their nests.

Barred owls and red-shouldered hawks are a different story. They'll nest near one another with no apparent conflict. In rare cases, they've been known to share the same nest.

However, barred owls do not extend the olive branch to other barred owls looking to move into their territory. The resident owls will aggressively defend their turf. Not surprisingly, barred owls are famous for their site loyalty. One pair returned to the same nest for over 30 years!

Camp OWL

Combine their site fidelity with their loquacious nature, and it is not surprising that barred owls have become forest icons.

Their woodland status was well described by Bishop Robert Hatch over fifty years ago. The Bishop spent one summer at Camp OWL located on a wooded New Hampshire hillside. The camp's name, coincidentally, was derived from the owners' initials.

The Bishop, an accomplished bird watcher, saw a wide variety of birds, including many birds of prey, during that summer. Yet, when all was said and done, it was the barred owl that ruled the woods.

I have watched red-tailed hawks circling over the camp, and one day I saw a goshawk as I sat on the porch. But none of these birds, not even the goshawk, could match the owl. Every night the hoots rang through the forest, now from this direction, now from that, until the owl seemed the master of these woods and all the other birds mere satellites.

BARRED OWL BASICS

Identifying Marks: Wingspan 38-50 inches; length 16-24 inches. Large, dark-eyed, gray-brown owl with a barred chest and striped belly. Unlike the somewhat larger great horned owl, the barred owl lacks "horns" or feather tufts on its head.

Range: From British Columbia across to Nova Scotia south throughout the eastern United States including all of Illinois, Wisconsin, and Indiana.

Nests: Tree cavities as well as abandoned nests of crows, squirrels, and hawks, especially red-shouldered hawks. The presence of large trees is key.

Diet: Mice, chipmunks, voles, shrews, insects (i.e. beetles, crickets, moths), snakes, lizards, frogs, toads, birds, and even an occasional fish.

SCREECHING OWLS

...the screetch-owl, screetching loud,
Puts the wretch that lies in woe
In remembrance of a shroud.

—William Shakespeare, *A Midsummer Night's Dream*

North American screech owls don't screech. O.K. they can, on a rare occasion, screech but then so can barred or great horned owls.

The characteristic screech owl call sounds like a descending quavering whinny or whistle. The bird also makes a soft tremolo or trilling sound. So why do we call it a screech owl rather than a whistling owl? Therein lies the beginning of this story.

The Bird of Avon

The opening quotation would suggest that screech owls *(Megascops asio)* can be found on Shakespeare's side of the Atlantic Ocean. In fact, what we call screech owls today can only be found on this side of the Atlantic.

So which owl's vocalization was Shakespeare describing? Lady MacBeth gives us some additional clues:

It was the owl that shriek'd,
the fatal bellman,
Which gives the stern'st good-night...
I heard the owls scream and the crickets cry.

Lady Macbeth was, no doubt, hearing a barn owl scream. The barn owl (*Tyto alba*), found on all continents except Antarctica, makes an assortment of loud abrasive shrieks, screeches, and hisses.

This owl's calls remind some of a brewing espresso coffee machine. Simply put, yesteryear's "screech owl" is today's barn owl.

The Name Game

How did our non-screeching owl get stuck with its inappropriate name? The same way the New World robin did. Let me explain.

Early settlers of this "new world" often named novel plants and animals after species from the old country, which brings us to the American robin.

When English settlers first saw our robin it reminded them of the robin redbreast of Europe and so it became a "robin."

Compared to our robin, the European original is much smaller with a patch of orange-red limited to the throat and chest.
It belongs to a different group of birds than ours. Of course, such details were unimportant to early colonists.

In a similar vein, while the New World screech owl is smaller, it did have some things in common with the Old World screech owl (aka barn owl). Both are nocturnal, both have eyes in front of their heads, and both share habitats with humans.

It has been suggested that in the early days, some might have heard a barn owl shriek when observing a screech owl.

Be that as it may, that our screech owl was named after the "original" screech owl makes sense to me.

Backyard Hunters

Today, one of the biggest differences between barn owls and screech owls is their relative abundance. Barn owls are endangered in Illinois while screech owls are quite common.

Wooded suburban and urban landscapes support healthy populations of screech owls all across the eastern two-thirds of the U. S. In fact, they seem to prefer these habitats. Eastern screech owl populations increase in proportion to the density of humans in urban areas.

In a 30-year Texas study, it was shown that suburban screech owls nested earlier and successfully raised more owlets than their counterparts nesting in agricultural habitats.

Also, urban screech owls defend relatively small territories. They can be just ten to fifteen acres in size. Compare that to the rural owls that have territories as large as seventy-five acres, nearly the size of our nature center.

The benefits of the urban-suburban lifestyle are many. Urban environs are often a bit warmer during the cold months. This is known as the "heat island effect."

Thanks to sprinklers, retention ponds, and so on, suburbia is more likely to have a constant water source available.

In addition, cities and suburbs, particularly older towns, are likely to have large trees. Since screech owls nest in natural cavities such as woodpecker holes, these trees are made to order. They'll also use nest boxes, by the way.

These man-made conditions not only benefit the owl but their prey as well. Anyone who has thought of calling a pest control service knows how many mice, chipmunks, insects, and other critters are living in your garage, under the porch, near your garden, or in a crawl space. With all this food concentrated in a small area, who needs a large territory?

The list of things this effective hunter eats is impressive. The owl's menu includes: moths, beetles, earthworms, cicadas, crayfish, spiders, lizards, mice, rats, bats, chipmunks, toads, doves, jays, robins, and sparrows.

Not bad for a bird that stands a little under nine inches tall. While I'm at it, the bird has a wingspan that is just over twenty inches.

The screech owl is the only small eastern owl with ear tufts. The surface of the upper wings is marked with white spots. This owl comes in different colors, including red and gray...but why?

Red vs. Gray

This question has been plaguing ornithologists for generations. Julio De La Torre wrote that the gray to red plumage of eastern screech owls could be explained, "as a conundrum of nature designed to keep Ph.D. candidates from running out of dissertation material."

Rest assured, I won't be resolving that question here. First, though, understand that "red" does not mean cardinal red but actually refers to more of a rust or rufous color.

Second, there are brownish screech owls that are intermediate along the gray to red gradient. Nearly all color varieties can be seen in northern Illinois.

Nationally, the red birds make up about a third of the eastern screech owl population. They avoid northern latitudes, preferring the warmer and more humid conditions in the eastern and southern portions of their range.

It turns out that rufous feathers are more susceptible to abrasion than gray feathers. So, drier environments can mean more feather damage for the red owls.

It is thought that perhaps the red feathers offer poorer insulation than gray plumage. Interestingly, red screech owls are more common in the slightly warmer and moist suburbs than in agricultural habitats.

Brief Lives

Whatever the color or habitat, eastern screech owls are not around for long. Every year, roughly seventy percent of the juveniles and thirty percent of the adults die. Causes of mortality range from road kills, window strikes, and poisoning to predators such as raccoons and weasels.

From the perspective of a short-lived nocturnal owl, those words from Lady MacBeth read differently:

It was the owl that shriek'd,
the fatal bellman,
Which gives the stern'st good-night...

TURKEY VULTURES: High-Death T.V.s

High on a rocky peak,
Jagged and scarred by thunder,
The solitary vulture sits with whetted beak
Gazing far under,
Over the desolate plain that lies beneath.
His cold eye glistens in the setting sun,
Watching until the fight be lost and won,
And silence reigns upon the field of death.

Prophet of evil! bird of omen, foul!
Unstained by living blood,
Corruption is thy food;
How man abhors thee, horrid ghoul!

    —Rev. T. C. Porter

This opening of Reverend Porter's nineteenth-century vulture poem does not exactly paint a pretty picture. In some areas, though, returning turkey buzzards are seen as harbingers of spring. Let's take a closer look at these increasingly common summer residents.

Is a vulture a buzzard?

It depends on where you are. If you are celebrating Buzzard Sunday in Hinckley, Ohio, you are welcoming the mid-March return of turkey vultures to the area. If you are photographing a jackal buzzard in S. Africa, you are not focusing on a vulture. Instead, you are zooming in on a buteo, a genus of hawks.

Buteo comes from the Latin *butes*, which refers to broad-winged hawks. This Latin term also gave rise to the old French word *busart*, which led to buzzard. So, for the most part, in the New World buzzard refers to a vulture while in the Old World it refers to a buteo. Of course, both buteos and vultures have broad wings.

Vulture wings, however, are much larger. The largest buteo commonly seen in our area, the red-tailed hawk, has a wingspan of approximately four feet. The turkey vulture measures close to six feet from wingtip to wingtip. In fact, the only raptorial bird large enough to confuse with a turkey vulture is a bald eagle.

So, if they are a long way off, how do you tell them apart? The flight profile, looking head on, of a bald eagle is flat. Turkey vultures hold their wings in a shallow 'V,' called a dihedral and similar to the wings of some hang gliders.

I can't help but think this wing arrangement is highly energy efficient, so to speak, as turkey vultures rarely flap their wings. Instead, they tilt and tip from side to side as if balancing on an unseen high wire.

Up close and very personal!

At close range, a turkey vulture won't be confused with any other bird of prey because, unlike a bald eagle, the vulture is really bald.

While a small red-skinned head is not particularly attractive, it is an example of form following function. Think about it. You make your living slurping down the guts of road-ripened raccoon, deer, rabbit, and opossum. When your head comes out of those rotting body cavities, it is covered with bacteria-laden slime.

Now, what kills bacteria? Ultra-violet light from the sun.

How to maximize the amount of sun hitting sticky skin? You got it, less feathers.

Not surprisingly, vultures are amazingly resistant to most diseases found in carrion such as botulism and salmonella.

As if these adaptations are interesting enough, let's move from the head end to the other end of a vulture. In birds, you see, feces and urine are combined and voided through a single opening or vent.

Why am I telling you this? Keep in mind that birds don't sweat. What good would sweat-soaked feathers be if you needed to fly away?

Now, picture our bare-headed and bare-legged vulture perched on a rocky ledge on an extremely hot day in, say, an Arizona desert. There's no water nearby and you need to cool down. What's the solution?

Well, the scientific term is urohidrosis. In other words, the bird directs the cloaca downward and forward to defecate on the legs or feet. Just as with sweat, the liquid feces evaporates and the vulture is cooled down. In addition, uric  acid in the poop helps kill germs on the vulture's feet. (Think about where those feet have been.) Neat, eh? Hmmm, maybe not so neat.

Short-legged Storks?

Interestingly, other groups of birds, such as boobies and storks, excrete on themselves to cool down. Traditionally, vultures were grouped with diurnal birds of prey based on their hooked beaks plus similar migratory and feeding habits. However, due to behavioral (i.e. urohidrosis) and genetic studies, their relationship to storks has been accepted.

The question that scientists are still wrestling with is when did our New World vultures split from the stork branch in the ornithological family tree? Suffice it to say, it was a long, long, time ago.

Dinner Smells

It should not come as a surprise that the turkey vultures have a great sense of smell. Even with their excellent eyesight, soaring vultures aren't going to be able to spot a dead raccoon if it is laying under a stand of trees, but they will smell it.

In fact, vultures have been attracted to stinkhorns, mushrooms that smell horrid. The stink attracts flies which land and then spread the mushrooms' sticky spores.

To be precise, the vulture-attracting gas emitted by carrion is ethyl mercaptan. When looking for leaks, at least one natural gas company has learned to introduce this odorant into pipelines. Then, all they have to do is look for where the vultures are circling.

Persecuted in the Past

The attitude expressed in Rev. Porter's poem led to unnecessary vulture deaths long after it was generally acknowledged that vultures are beneficial scavengers. During the early to mid-1900s, for instance, Texas ranchers killed over 100,000 black and turkey vultures.

Given their ability to smell rotting meat, vultures also ran afoul of poisoned baits and leg-hold traps set out for various other predators. But, Rev. Porter knew the truth. His vulture poem continues:

> *And yet thou art a minister of God*
> *To rid the world of pestilence and taint;*
> *Thou sparest both the sinner and the saint*
> *Under the sod.*

HEARTLAND HABITATS: Raptors in the Land of Lincoln

"Welcome to the Land of Lincoln," read the highway signs. Welcome to Illinois where, as the old joke goes, the roads leave you ill and annoyed. Actually, the roads here, like the roads in Iowa, Kansas, and elsewhere in the heartland, generally lead you through three types of human-made landscapes: agricultural, urban, and the tension zone between the first two, the suburbs.

Few traveling nature lovers make Illinois their vacation destination. Those of us who live and work here know that if you're willing to look, wildlife can be found. I don't mean resilient species such as the carp or pigeon, but spectacular predatory birds such as the great horned owl, peregrine falcon, and bald eagle. Of these three, the most stealthy, most efficient killer, and most feared is the great horned owl. On a frigid night in January of this year, an interesting coincidence drove this point home.

Affluent Food Chain

Like many Americans, I call suburbia home. My particular suburb is an affluent one, located northwest of Chicago. Many of my neighbors live in huge houses with manicured lawns and sensitive security systems. It's the kind of community that is likely to report to the police the sight of a fellow wandering around the neighborhood with binoculars. That fellow with the binoculars is me, and I wander around the neighborhood almost every day.

I can get away with this behavior because I live and work on an old 80-acre estate that was willed to become a nature center. Surrounded on all sides by housing developments, this nature center, with its small pond, tiny pine plantation, overgrown orchard, and new prairie, is an island of open space enjoyed by many animals.

At the top of this nature center's food chain sits the great horned owl. Our resident owls were busily hooting on a chilly January evening as I contemplated a news clipping. The AP story described a great horned owl seen in Greenville, Maine, that allegedly "lifted the twenty-pound poodle-pekingese mix into the air and out of sight."

Come again? An owl that averages about four pounds in weight carries a twenty-pound dog into the sky? I found that difficult to believe, especially in light of experiments showing that much larger birds, such as the golden eagle, would be unable to carry such a weight.

As the owls outside my window continued to hoot, I was reminded of stories from earlier in the century about eagles carrying off children. I also recalled an exchange between a neighbor and one of our nature center's board members. Apparently, a neighbor had called the board member to complain that "our coyotes" were likely to get one of his pets. The board member responded that the culprit would more likely be an owl. Why is it so easy to make owls the villains? I grabbed my binoculars and went outside.

As I walked, it wasn't long before I spotted one of two hooting owls. It was perched on a tall snag, about thirty feet overhead. This snag was a monument to our center's changing nature. At one time, a large silver maple grew next to the estate's mansion. The top of the tree died and it was feared that the tree would collapse and fall into the roof. So, the dead top was removed, leaving a large, decapitated tree with live side branches. As time passed, neighboring trees and fields were giving way to houses and garages. On the estate, however, the reverse happened. The mansion was removed and the tree remained, the tree that was now a perch for a hooting great horned owl.

The sun had set, yet from my position in a clearing, the binoculars gathered enough light for me to see the owl's face clearly. It was staring directly at me with its ominous-looking yellow eyes arranged on the front of its head, much like human eyes. I guess it isn't so difficult to see why the great horned owl, with its rotating head and gargoyle-like stature, is the raptor people love to hate (see front cover).

Finding the second owl, on the other hand, was not so easy. I was making my way through some shrubs in hopes of seeing the other bird when the hooting duet was interrupted by an unearthly scream. Although I have rarely heard this call, I knew it was a great horned owl, but which one? One of the two I had been hearing, or was it an interloper?

I returned to the clearing in time to see the male owl perched on the rump of the bowing female, keeping his position with flapping, outstretched wings. After a brief mating effort, he flew off to the pines as she perched upright on the snag, swiveling her head and calmly surveying her surroundings. This is *their* home, I thought. They live their lives all around us; eating, mating, and raising their young.

The owls' habitat isn't limited to just the nature center grounds. They hunt for food in suburban yards where their human neighbors raise their own young and eat their own food. We both use the environment, but given the owl's abundance in suburban and urban areas, I can't help but conclude that it is less concerned with us than we are with it, especially when we hear the owl's blood-curdling scream in the middle of the night.

Aerial Muggings

In Chicago, birds and muggers often occupy the same habitat. Shrubs conceal both two-legged migrants and two-legged purse snatchers. Years ago, high above the concealing hedges, I watched another form of avian mugging: the stoops of endangered peregrine falcons. The peregrines, part of a nationwide restoration effort, were first released from the roof of a University of Illinois building on Chicago's near West Side. Decades earlier, the University had been carved out of an ethnic neighborhood. Controversy and protest surrounded its arrival. Similarly, the peregrines' arrival inspired protest.

Hostile cries first emanated from the city's pigeon enthusiasts. The falcons' spectacular stoops on hapless pigeons and chimney swifts went unseen at street level, and human objections quickly faded. Other high-rise residents, however, were still vocal about the endangered newcomers.

To better understand this dispute, we need to view Chicago from a peregrine observation post located on top of a fifty-story building. In an odd way, going up in the city is like going north for the weekend.

An unusual sense of serenity and wilderness is experienced while observing urban life from the heights of human-made cliffs. There is a surprising assortment of wildlife crawling over or flying by concrete ledges. Ladybugs, butterflies, and, on one memorable day, thousands of ballooning spiderlings all joined me on my building perch.

Of course, there were birds. The peregrines dined on starlings, robins, woodpeckers, jays, and a variety of migrating warblers. Contrary to popular news accounts, peregrines were not the first predaceous falcons to call the city home. Kestrels had long ago staked out their turf and, as I learned, they weren't about to put out the welcome mat for their larger cousins.

In fact, one of the first flights made by a young peregrine drew a kestrel's fire. A peregrine's early flight rarely includes one of their famous 180-mile-per-hour dives. More than likely, it involves one of their less than famous clumsy landings. As a peregrine observer, I was concerned that our rare fledglings avoid reflective glass and open chimneys, but I had not anticipated an aerial assault.

Shortly after the peregrine launched itself from a twenty-eight-story ledge, I heard the kestrel's familiar call, *"killy, killy, killy, killy, killy."* An interesting coincidence, I thought, as I watched the peregrine glide across the Eisenhower expressway. Abruptly, he collapsed his wings, dropped a few feet, and began flapping in the direction of an old water tower located on the roof of a brick warehouse. The cause of his haste was a coppery-blue blur that repeatedly buzzed the lumbering falcon.

Now I understood the meaning of the kestrel's angry cries: "Get out of here! Beat it! This town isn't big enough for two species from the same genus!"

As the nesting of mature peregrines later showed, Chicago *is* big enough for both species of falcons. Life in the city is tough, though, and dead falcons are occasionally found. So far, the pesticides that nearly extirpated peregrines in the past have not caused the more recent deaths. Thanks to tighter regulations on pesticide use, not only peregrines but bald eagles as well have been able to enjoy a comeback.

Christmas Ham

In Illinois, a winter trip through fallow fields and aromatic pig farms can lead to a surprising sight of a well-attended conference of bald eagles with representatives from throughout the upper Midwest. Without human interference, these eagle get-togethers would be difficult. The advocates of endangered fishes and mussels may hate dams, but eagles love them. During severe winters when the Mississippi River freezes over, the turbulent waters beneath the dams remain open. Since fish are at the top of the bald eagle's menu, the birds often gather in great numbers at dam sites.

It took me two trips before I made it to the dam along the Mississippi River at the Quad Cities. During the first attempt, I got stranded in Kewanee, boiler capital of the world and not my intended goal. A friend and I had decided to shun the interstate in favor of smaller roads. After that, our itinerary was in the hands of a Midwestern blizzard.

When the snow falls and the wind blows across the barren farmlands of the heartland, very little stands in the way. To make matters worse, there's little to keep the ground itself from blowing away. That evening, we had hoped to arrive at the river. Our choice of roads, blizzard white-out conditions, and impassable drifts of snow and soil landed us at a motel in Kewanee.

During the night temperatures dropped well below zero. The next morning my Swedish car showed uncharacteristic Scandinavian reserve and refused to start. Eventually, with the help of some wiring borrowed from the Coke machine, the car shook off the chill and turned over. We followed a slow procession of vehicles led by three huge snow plows that punctured, pushed, and cleared the drifts ahead of us, drifts that had engulfed abandoned cars and trailers.

At one point, 1 did notice a couple of eagles in a field near a farm composed of many low sheds. As it turned out, those were the only eagles we saw. By the time we reached a cleared expressway, our work schedules required us to return to Chicago.

A few days later, with another acquaintance in tow, I tried again. It was a mild weekend, steam rose above frozen fields and fog-shrouded creek bottoms. We started spotting eagles along the highway long before reaching the outskirts of Rock Island and the Quad Cities. Their proximity to the road reminded me of a past trip through Wyoming when I spotted a pair of eagles feeding on a road-killed pronghorn antelope. It made sense. Where better to find a free lunch than along I-80? They're nothing more than slow-flapping crows with white heads, I thought.

It wasn't an original thought. Years ago, Benjamin Franklin had obviously made similar observations when he accused our national symbol of being "a bird of bad moral character. .. who does not get his living honestly."

As we continued through the countryside, I saw farms with buildings like those I had seen on my previous trip. Their distinctive and over-powering odor identified them as pig farms. Eagles at pig farms?

We finally reached the Mississippi and in the shadow of an aging armory, watched a handful of eagles perched in a cluster of trees, sulking as a light rain fell. The warm weather had led to an early ice breakup and many eagles had dispersed along the river, away from the dam. Nonetheless, the sight of a dozen eagles was an encouraging sign. "These are the best-looking eagles I've seen by a dam sight," my friend quipped.

Another positive sign was the community's awareness of the eagles' activities. Cynics would suggest that the community is not interested in eagles but in the contents of eagle watchers' wallets. I'm sure that this is often the case, but haven't the interests of professional wildlife managers been dictated by hunters' dollars?

I made a few inquiries about the eagles I had seen at a pig farm and had my suspicions confirmed. Apparently, some farmers dispose of their dead pigs by simply dumping them in the "lower 40." Our Midwestern eagles don't seem to mind a chilled Christmas ham. Ben Franklin had them pegged all along.

Wild Lives

Perhaps you'd rather watch your eagles in northern Minnesota. That's a *real* wilderness experience, right? I suppose, if you don't think about acid rain or the advisories concerning the chemical levels in the fish that eagles eat.

Maybe you'd rather spot peregrines at a cliff nest in northern California. After all, those are "wild" falcons, right? I guess so, but even at the end of the twentieth century those peregrines were having a tough time reproducing. It seems their eggs still had high levels of dioxin and PCB. Like the range of the omnipresent great horned owl, no place is free from human influence.

So, welcome to Illinois, land of eagle, owl, falcon, and Lincoln. Perhaps we lack the wilderness settings offered by other states. Maybe our owls hunt in suburban yards, our eagles feed on farmers' leftovers, and our peregrines nest on bank buildings, but they're survivors. They have adapted their wild lives to our domestic ones, and we are the richer for it. Travel to the wilderness if you must, but when you are ready for an honest wildlife experience, stop by the heartland or just look around your suburb or city. Wildlife lives there. Allegedly pristine settings are not prerequisites to wildlife adventures.

It is, in large part, up to you. Remember, it's not the habitat; it's the attitude.

OWLS: Harbingers of Death

It was the owl that shriek'd, the fatal bellman,
Which gives the stern'st good-night...
I heard the owl shrieking and the crickets cry.

—Macbeth, Act II, Sc. 2

That owls are familiar Halloween icons is just the latest incarnation of a human fascination with owls that predates recorded history. One of the oldest illustrations of a bird that can be identified to species is a drawing of a snowy owl that was scratched on a wall in a French cave at least 20,000 years old. Because this cave was used by early humans as a sanctuary, it is believed that these birds symbolized religious or magical powers.

Symbol of Doom?

These powers might have included warning humans of an impending death. The owl's association with doom can be traced back to the Mesopotamian goddess of Death, Lilith, who was typically flanked by owls. Along with her owl entourage, a Sumerian tablet of 2,300 - 2,000 B.C. shows Lilith with wings, talons in place of toes, and sporting a headdress of horns.

It is likely that these ancient Middle East beliefs influenced the early Greeks because the owl became the symbol of Pallas Athena, the Greek goddess of wisdom and warfare. Athenians believed their warrior goddess would sometimes help them on the battlefield. In the battle of Marathon against the Persians, the Athenians believed Athena assumed the form of an owl and led them to victory from overhead.

Around 77 B.C., Pliny the Elder, a Roman scholar, and author of *Historia Naturalis*, collected information about a variety of subjects, including owls. He tried to dispel the notion that an owl was symbolic of doom. He wrote that, on more than one occasion, he had seen an owl perched on a private house and had later learned that nothing untoward had happened to any of the house's occupants. Public places, however, were a different matter. Pliny wrote that the "owle betokeneth always some heavy news, and is most execrable and accursed in the presaging of public affairs...."

During the Middle Ages, the early Christian church saw the owl as the perfect symbol of evil. After all, it is a creature of darkness, makes a haunting sound, perches upright not unlike a standing human, and stares at you with two piercing yellow eyes that are arranged, much like ours, on the front of its head. What a perfect little demon!

Shakespeare often used the owl as a bird of ill-omen. In Macbeth, for example, at the moment her husband is about to kill King Duncan, Lady Macbeth speaks the opening quotation to this article.

On this side of the Atlantic, the owl was viewed as a harbinger of death as well. According to a tribal elder of the Oto-Missouri tribe:

The owl is the one that gives the death warning.
The owl that's got the horns they are the ones that warn you. ...
Hear them in the distance, it never fails, never fails, death is close.

Raptor Warriors

It should not be surprising to learn that, here in Illinois, owl bones have been found as grave offerings in sites of the prehistoric Mississippian culture.

Some Sierra tribes of California believed that the great horned owl, one of those "that's got the horns," seized the souls of the dead and transported them to the other world. Also from the West Coast, the Newuk Indians believed that the virtuous among them became great horned owls while the wicked were cursed to become barn owls.

Much as Athena's owl did at Marathon, a Pima Chief describes how an owl aided his tribe against the Apaches:

...[the owl] looked about and saw my plan...
He cut the power of the enemy, their springs, their trees, their dreams
He bit off their flesh and sinews, and made holes in their bones

In Athens, the little owl was common in the city and another source of inspiration for owl folklore. In the Western Hemisphere, we have a close relative of Athena's bird, the burrowing owl. Since it nests in old prairie dog burrows, this owl is, in a literal sense, of the underworld.

Underworld Fertility

The association of the burrowing owl with doom was made by the Hopi Indians who identified this bird with their god of the dead, Masau'u. However, being this god's symbol was not necessarily a bad thing. Masau'u's realm included all things under the ground. So, the burrowing owl's deity was also in charge of germinating seeds

and growing crops. All in all, the owl was smiled upon by the Hopi.
Can a bird of darkness and the underworld be a source of humor?
Yes, according to W.H. Davies, whose poem concludes this article.
In the meantime, if you're out on Halloween and hear an owl hooting,
don't worry. It has nothing to say about your future... or does it?

The boding Owl, that in despair
Doth moan and shiver on warm nights—
Shall this bird prophesy for me
The fall of Heavens eternal lights?
When in the thistled field of Age
I take my final walk on earth,
Still will I make that Owl's despair
A thing to fill my heart with mirth.

Snapping turtle photo by Mark Spreyer.

VI. AQUATICS

A lake is the landscape's most beautiful and expressive feature. It is Earth's eye; looking into which the beholder measures the depth of his own nature.

— Henry David Thoreau

FROGS OF PREY

Traditionally, the phrase *birds of prey* refer to birds, such as hawks and eagles, that seize their food with their talons. However, these are not the only predatory birds. Whether it's a robin slurping down a worm or a kingfisher diving on a fish, there are many birds that feed on other animals.

Let's stop right here. Do you feel sorry for the worm or the fish? Probably not. Now, let's turn the table. Instead of a warm-blooded, feathery bird eating a cold-blooded fish or worm, what if a cold-blooded creature eats a warm-blooded, baby bird? Well, it happened here at the nature center in front of a group of fourth-graders.

Setting the Stage

Late in May, fourth graders from a nearby elementary school were on their first field trip to Stillman. As is our custom, we divided the group in two. Half start with a walk and then do pond study while the other half start at the pond and then walk through the woods.

As I was bringing the first group to the pond, a pair of startled wood ducks took off leaving their newly hatched chicks behind. Almost all of the ducklings headed east but one dumb duck hung around. I thought for sure, once the kids got started with the nets, this wayward duck would catch up with the other ducklings.

No such luck. As the fourth graders reached into the water with long-handled dip nets, the wood duckling headed our way. Sure enough he came on shore and all the students were very excited to see the little guy. I told the kids that it would be best if "junior" joined his siblings back in the lake.

So, I picked him up and headed east around the building to our other dock. Here, I ran into the other half of the school group which was about to trade activities with my group. I explained the situation, released the wayward duckling in sight of its nest mates and the children, then headed back to finish up with the first pond study class.

Frogzilla

A couple of minutes later, the second group arrived and did they have a predatory story to tell. Shortly after I left the dumb duckling to find his mates, a large bullfrog found "junior." The frog came from under the duckling and swallowed it from behind.

As one of the adult chaperones explained it to me, the last thing that was seen was the head of the peeping duckling being pulled under by frogzilla. This graphic demonstration of the food chain had an impact on the audience. Here's a sampling from the students' thank you letters:

> *That little chick was cool until it got eaten.*
> *The funniest part of all and sad at the same time is* [sic] *when the bull frog ate the baby duckling...*
> *I sure hope the violence that happened doesn't happen anymore.*
> *I really enjoyed everything. I learned about the food chain (even though you didn't plan to teach us that).*

Actually, I did.
For obvious reasons, though, I'm more likely to talk about plant-eating ducks and bug-eating birds then puppy-eating alligators and bird-eating frogs. Hey, there's a  reason that Hollywood has had such success scaring us with aquatic, cold-blooded predators (i.e. *Anaconda, Jaws* 1 - 27, etc.).

As you can tell, this incident gave me a chance to revisit the food chain. Specifically, as Thomas Tyning wrote in his guide to amphibians and reptiles, "Don't be shocked if you see a bullfrog going after 'unfroglike' meals. They are known to eat mice, small turtles, fish, snakes, birds, and other frogs...."

I was also reminded that nature shows no favorites, warm-blooded or cold-blooded, and has no mercy. Whether you're at the top, at the bottom, or in the middle— we are all just links in the food chain. As John Burroughs wrote, "Nature is not benevolent; Nature is just, gives pound for pound, measure for measure, makes no exceptions, never tempers her decrees with mercy, or winks at any infringement of her laws."

BIG AND LITTLE TURTLE

A long, long time ago, before there were any people or any earth, according to an Iroquois legend, the gods lived above the sky and below was nothing but water populated by animals such as swans, muskrats, turtles and toads. One day, two swans were swimming on the water when they heard a thundering noise and looked up to see a Sky Woman falling through a hole in the sky.

The swans caught her in their wings but realized that she could not live in the water and they could not hold her up forever. They called a meeting of the water animals to decide what to do.

Big Turtle said, "If someone will dive down into the water and bring up some earth from below, I will hold the earth on my back and we shall have land for Sky Woman to live on."

So the water animals took turns diving. Muskrat tried but could not find the earth below. Beaver made a deep dive but did not reach the mud. And so it went.

Finally, Little Toad tried. He was gone so long that the other animals thought he would never come up. When at last he surfaced, his mouth was full of earth. The animals took the earth and spread it all over Big Turtle's back.

When this was done, a marvelous thing happened. The amount of earth grew larger and larger until Big Turtle had all of North America on his back.

Sky Woman was happy with her new home but there was no light and she had a difficult time finding her way in the darkness. The animals again met in council.

"Let me go up to the sky," Little Turtle said, "I will put a light there for the Sky Woman."

Then, a great thundercloud rolled over the waters and Little Turtle jumped into the cloud and rode up to the sky. He snatched some of the lightning out of the cloud and rolled it into a ball which he fastened to the roof of the heavens. In this way, Little Turtle made the sun in the sky.

Painted Turtles

There are, of course, other versions of this Native American creation story but I am particularly fond of this one because here at the nature center, you can see almost all these water animals. As I type this, a muskrat swims along the shore of the pond. And, do we have turtles! This spring, students have counted as many as 35 turtles basking on one fallen tree. These 35 were all painted turtles *(Chrysemys picta)* or, what I like to think of as Little Turtle's descendants.

In fact, painted turtles are little, ranging in length from 4.5 to 7 inches. Males are smaller than females and, when mature, can be recognized by the long nails on their forefeet.

Two different subspecies are found here in northern Illinois, the midland and western painted turtles. All painted turtles have an olive-green *carapace,* or upper shell portion, and a yellow to red lower shell, called the *plastron.* The western is the largest of the painted turtles and has an intricate, dark pattern on its orange plastron.

As mentioned earlier, these turtles are commonly seen basking together. A period of basking usually lasts about two hours. Basking is most frequent from April through September and peaks in the morning. In northern regions, morning basking is probably necessary to raise this coldblooded reptile's body temperature to operational levels.

Once at those levels, the turtles forage for food. They are generalists which dine on a wide variety of plants and animals including algae, duckweed, leeches, slugs, crayfish, dead fish, tadpoles, beetles, water striders plus larval mayflies, damselflies and mosquitoes.

When watching painted turtles basking on a log, I can't help but wonder if they know that they are enjoying the warm benefits of Little Turtle's efforts. Perhaps their plastrons are orange because a little part of the sun that their ancestor formed remains stuck to their shells.

Snapping Turtles

If the latter is so, then part of the earth is still clinging to the back of today's Big Turtle, the snapping turtle *(Chelydra serpentina)*. How big is big? Their shells are 8 to 12 inches in length and weights of 10 to 35 pounds are common in the wild. A fattened captive specimen tipped the scales at 86 pounds. The length measurements do not include the head (see page 160) or long, saw-toothed tail.

Unlike painted turtles, snapping turtles rarely bask and when they do, they do it alone. Instead, a snapper likes to rest in muddy shallows, with only its eyes and nostrils exposed.

Under the water, a snapper is usually shy, swimming away or just pulling its head in when disturbed. However, if encountered on land or lifted from the water, watch out! It will strike repeatedly and can inflict a serious bite.

Its choice of foods is only limited by what fits into its jaws. A study in Michigan found that the snapper's diet was 37% plants and 54% animals by volume. A partial list of the animals consumed includes spiders, snails, crabs, clams, leeches, snakes, birds, salamanders, small turtles plus the eggs, young and adults of various fish, frogs and toads. Carrion is also eaten.

A young turtle will actively seek out food while an older snapper simply waits and ambushes its prey. Small items are swallowed whole while larger prey is held in the mouth and scraped with the strong foreclaws into more manageable pieces. Feeding usually takes place underwater.

The images of these plated, primitive reptiles does suggest a wetland version of Jurassic Park. Perhaps Big Turtle does still carry the continent on his shell. If so, Californians take note. Big Turtle grows weary of his massive load from time to time and will move his shell to shift the weight. That's why the earth quakes.

NO *CARP*ING ZONE

Normally, in this space, I feature an animal or plant that can be found here at the nature center. To this date, I have never seen a carp in either our lake or marsh. However, since this fish is so common in nearby lakes and rivers, I thought you might be interested in learning more about it. Even though I'm an Illinois native, I did not truly appreciate carp until I lived in Minnesota, near the famous northern lake country, home to popular fish species such as the walleye or northern pike.

There, I met pair of Minnesotans who, despite their proximity to pristine lakes, were dedicated to convincing anglers that the much-maligned carp is the REAL challenge for fishermen. These Minnesotans, Rob Buffler and Tom Dickson, have written a book, *Fishing for Buffalo,* in which they argue that many overlooked species of fish, including the carp, should be appreciated and enjoyed rather than ignored or shunned.

Before proceeding to the carp's conquest of North America, let's take a closer look at this remarkable fish. The common carp, a thick-bodied fish with an arching back, can reach four feet in length. It has a brassy olive back, lighter sides, and is yellowish below. The carp is one of the larger members of the Minnow Family.

Carp have a rather unusual mouth. Two pairs of barbels are found at the corner of the mouth. In the carp, the rear pair of these fleshy projections are more noticeable and suggest the fish is wearing a droopy moustache over its protruding, down-turned mouth. In its throat, it has pharyngeal teeth that allow it to grind up mollusks, crustaceans and other invertebrates that are protected by crusty exoskeletons.

So, how did the non-native carp arrive in North America? After the Civil War, the federal government turned its attention to the country's natural resources. Thanks to unregulated commercial fishing operations, fish were becoming increasingly scarce at East Coast markets. In addition, garbage, sewage and the other by-products of human settlements were simply flushed into the nearest river. The waters' increased turbidity, temperature, and bacteria levels made existence precarious for those fish that had escaped the fishermen's nets and seines.

At the same time native fish were disappearing, human immigrants were asking that carp be brought to America. Because of its widespread popularity in Europe, Germans, Scandinavians, French and other nationalities had all grown accustomed to consuming carp. When they learned that this country lacked carp, they did what concerned citizens often do, they wrote the government. Their letters landed on Spencer Baird's desk.

Baird was in charge of the United States Commission of Fish and Fisheries which was formed by President Grant in 1871. After a few fish fact-finding tours in Europe, Baird arranged for a shipment of carp which arrived on our shores in 1877. By 1883, 260,000 fish were distributed to almost every one of the country's 301 congressional districts. After the carp arrived at their various destinations, Baird continued to get letters. Many included glowing endorsements like this from Texan Sam Johnson,

> *My carp which you sent me...are doing well. They grow like China*
> *pigs when fed with plenty of buttermilk.*

As the years went by, people had second thoughts about their carp. The once· prized immigrant was, and continues to be, accused of muddying the waters and driving off more desirable species of fish. One might wonder, though, what came first, the carp or the mud?

Water pollution was not in the vocabulary of nineteenth century America. Had it been, people might have recognized that the carp was not the cause of the country's declining water quality. On the other hand, the carp was new, it was foreign, and it did have some messy habits.

Whether in streams or lakes, carp activities had an impact. Their constant vacuuming for food would sometimes cause aquatic vegetation to be uprooted. This combined with their vigorous spawning action could result in a muddier or more turbid lake. To the human European immigrants, it was an open and shut case. As Buffler and Dickson write, the settlers "saw carp swirling happily in the mess humans had created, and made a correlation--albeit the wrong one— between the rise of carp and the fall of game fish."

Now we know that the carp is not the villain it has been made out to be. Buffler and Dickson state,

> *In most lakes, carp reach a balance with other fish species. Most*
> *fisheries scientists who've studied carp agree that changes in land*
> *use have hurt game fish more than carp ever could.*

They continue,

> *We've seen carp swimming happily in clean wilderness streams*
> *and in smelly urban rivers. Although carp thrive in turbid, polluted*

*water, the fact that they do well in the waters where humans store
their garbage reflects the species' tolerance, not its preference.*

Furthermore, carp are helping to control another exotic species, the zebra mussel. According to a report from the National Biological Survey, 26 of 31 carp taken from the Mississippi River near St. Louis had zebra mussels in their stomachs. One of the carp contained 204 mussels! Thanks to the carp's pharyngeal teeth, the mussel shells found in the fish stomachs were crushed and well-fragmented.

Promoting carp may sound difficult but it is the pragmatic way to proceed. The only way to effectively limit carp would be much too expensive. As George C. Becker writes in *Fishes of Wisconsin:*

> *Unless we are willing to spend millions of dollars to pull out dams and restore the watersheds of our streams ... we will have carp in abundance.*

BEAVER AND HUMAN COLONIES

The works of the beaver have ever intensely interested the human mind. Beaver works may do for children what schools, sermons, companions and even home sometimes fail to do — develop the power to think.

—from *In Beaver World* by Enos Mills (1913)

Now that beavers have set up shop here at the nature center, I thought it would be interesting to trace their history in North America. With that in mind, I can't think of a better historical guide than Enos Mills.

Born in 1870, Mills was a dedicated conservationist who settled in Estes Park, Colorado. Once there, he worked tirelessly for the creation of Rocky Mountain National Park that was established by Congress in 1915. The Denver Post dubbed him "The Father of Rocky Mountain National Park."

As the opening quotation suggests, he was also an author. As you might expect, *In Beaver World* is set in what is now the National Park.

In 1991, I reviewed *In Beaver World* (which had been reissued by the University of Nebraska Press) for a couple of environmental publications. I shared the review with a friend who was a ranger at the Park. He, in turn, shared it with a member of his congregation, Enda (yes, Enda) Mills, Enos' daughter.

Beavers in Illinois

A hundred years ago, when Enos Mills was watching his Colorado beavers, they had been nearly or entirely exterminated here in

Illinois. At one time, they were common in the state.

In describing his second trip to Illinois (1674-1675), Father Marquette said that the local Indians gave beaver skins as gifts. Before the interior, low-lying areas of Illinois were drained, beavers were present. Early settlers in Champaign County found beavers and beaver dams.

In the 1700's, an inventory for one Illinois trapper indicated that he had taken 4,443 pounds of beaver. Keep in mind that a beaver typically ranges in weight from 26 to 60 pounds. In 1819, 199 beaver pelts passed through the Fort Edwards trading post in Illinois' Hancock County.

Money, of course, was the reason why the animals were relentlessly trapped. In 1831, beavers taken along the Rock and Mississippi rivers were worth two dollars a pound.

Ninety years ago, Mills saw what was happening, "In the golden age of the beaver, their countless colonies clustered all over our land." He continues, "Elm avenues now arch where the low-growing willow drooped across the [beaver-dug] canal, and a populous village stands upon the seat of a primitive and forgotten colony." Mills would be surprised to learn that in many of our suburbs today, a healthy beaver might be easier to find than a thriving elm.

How did the beavers return to Illinois? With a little help from Uncle Sam. As early as 1929, the U.S. Fish and Wildlife Service released a pair on the Savanna Army Depot.

In the 1930's, the Forest Service also sponsored beaver releases in Illinois while other beavers were being stocked in Missouri. In the 1940's, they were released along the Mississippi River in Iowa. Other beavers, no doubt, came on their own from neighboring states.

Just the Facts

In case you're wondering, adult beavers range in length from three to four feet. This measurement includes the famous tail.

Their diet includes the bark and cambium (growing layer) of shrubs and trees. In summer, they eat more herbaceous material such as grasses, duckweed, and other aquatic plants (i.e. water lily roots).

Beavers breed once a year in January or February. Typically there are three to four kits in a litter. They are weaned in two months.

Beaver stick lodges are four to ten feet high and twelve to thirty feet in diameter. Lodges can contain an adult pair as well as kits of the year and yearlings. Once reaching two years of age, parents give their young the boot... or tail, I should say. Bank burrows, such as we had here at the nature center, usually contain only one or two beavers.

O.K., back to the story.

Problems with your Neighbors?

Beavers are now so plentiful that some villages are trapping them because they are cutting residents' trees. Good luck with the trapping. In a Tennessee study, 169 resident beavers were removed from a wetland site. Within a few years, 162 new beavers had moved in. Migrating two-year-olds, in search of new territory, often move into vacated ponds and lodges.

The Village Forester for a nearby community has noted this pattern in her village. A few years ago, beavers were gnawing trees along a stream connected to a lake in her town. Homeowners hired trappers. Beaver activity ceased for a couple of years. Now, she has noticed the tell-tale (or should that be tail-tale?) signs of beaver in the very same area.

Protecting the more valuable trees would be a better solution. I suggest stopping at a hardware store and buying a roll of heavy gauge wire mesh (4 feet high with 2" by 4" squares). Form a cylinder with the wire and place it around the tree. Leave about five to six inches between the tree and the freestanding cylinder. As long as the wire is flush with the ground, the beaver should not go under it.

Back to Colorado

Since reviewing *In Beaver World*, I've had a chance to visit with Enda Mills. Despite being only three when her father died in 1922, she has done an honorable job of looking after his cabin in the Rockies and keeping his memory alive.

It is a sense of history that our nature center's beavers inspire in me. As Mills correctly observed, "The beaver hastened, if it did not bring, the settlement of the country." Voyageurs, and the fur companies behind them, opened pathways and established trading posts across the continent. When the supply of beavers was exhausted, the settlements often remained.

Now, the once-rare beavers are colonizing our human landscapes. Somehow, that only seems appropriate.

Story Update: *Since this article was first published, our beavers have sought lodging elsewhere. Enda Kiley (Mills) died in 2009.*

CRUSTACEANS AND CAJUNS: A Closer Look at Crayfish

You get a line and I get a pole, now honey
You get a line and I get a pole, babe,
You get a line and I get a pole,
We'll go down to the crawdad hole,
Honey oh babe of mine.

—Traditional Song

If the word crustacean reminds you of something you scraped off a boat once, you'd be right. Barnacles are crustaceans along with water fleas, shrimp, crabs, lobsters and crayfish.

Crustacean comes from the Latin word meaning "hard shell" and these animals are characterized by a tough exoskeleton along with numerous jointed legs.

Earlier today (this being the second week in May), a visiting school class caught many young crayfish during our pond study class. So let's get down to the crayfish, I mean, crawdad hole and take a closer look.

Acadian Legend

Being a relative of the lobster, crawdads are often on the menu, particularly in Louisiana, where it is the state crustacean. How did Cajuns get so fond of their crayfish? That's a story that goes back centuries, to the Acadians.

The Acadians were French settlers of eastern Canada. There they lived and fished for cod, herring and their favorites, lobsters.

In the early 1700s, the British took control of Canada and the Acadians headed south for Louisiana, a French territory.

As you can imagine, these folks were sad to go but, as you might not be aware, the lobsters were sorry to see them leave. So, the lobsters decided to follow them by crawling along on the ocean's bottom.

It was a tough, long journey for the Acadians and the lobsters. When they arrived in Louisiana, both groups of refugees had lost a lot of weight and were much more wiry than they used to be. The Acadians settled back in the freshwater swamps and the little lobsters followed along.

The lobsters watched as the French refugees built their homes in the swamps. While they had plenty of wood for walls and roofs, they had no stone to use for a fireplace or chimney. They needed a safe fireplace in order to prepare all that fine Acadian food.

Well, the tiny lobsters had an idea. It wasn't long before the Acadians noticed how their little multi-legged friends built chimneys out of mud. Soon, their cabins were outfitted with mud fireplaces and chimneys.

Names change over time and soon the Acadians were known as Cajuns and the little lobsters had their French moniker simplified to crayfish or crawdad. And, to this day, the Cajuns still love their crawdads!

Pincers & Burrows

They got two big claws and eight tiny feet, now honey
Two big claws and eight tiny feet, now babe,
Two big claws and eight tiny feet,
A tail full of meat that's good to eat,
Honey oh babe of mine.

Yes, the song's right. Crayfish belong to a group of crustaceans known as the Decapoda meaning ten feet.

The first two legs carry large pincers that the crawdads use to excavate their burrows. Burrows in water, you ask? Yes and no.

Crawfish generally are found in lakes, streams, marshes and other wet areas. However, some of these wet refuges are temporary ponds and pools that dry out during warmer weather. Since crayfish filter oxygen through gills, the little crustaceans must maintain some contact with water.

Here in northern Illinois, three species solve this problem by digging burrows. Given that they have to reach the water table, these burrows can be quite deep. Is it any wonder that crayfish pincers push up noticeable "chimneys" of excavated soil?

Predator or Protector?

The crawdad's large claws are also used to catch their prey that includes a wide variety of plants and animals, dead or alive. Some crayfish are particularly fond of snails. Their idea of escargot includes eating the shells which help strengthen their exoskeleton.

Interestingly, laboratory and field studies indicate that crayfish can significantly reduce populations of exotic zebra mussels living in streams.

Back to the pond study class mentioned earlier. When introducing the activity, I explain to the students that adult dragonflies eat adult mosquitoes in the air while dragonfly larvae, which use gills to breathe, eat mosquito larvae in the lake.

If given a chance, the omnivorous crayfish will snack on dragonfly larvae. Now if you are researching the endangered Hine's emerald dragonfly here in northern Illinois, you might be unhappy to see crawfish chimneys turning up in your dragonfly study area. Think again.

Researchers from the Illinois Natural History Survey and the University of Illinois discovered that during dry periods, the larvae of the endangered dragonfly took refuge in the wet crayfish burrows.

As water levels dropped, the density of dragonfly larvae in crayfish burrows showed much lower fluctuations than those in a stream channel.

In addition, field experiments showed that if the crayfish were removed, the abundance of Hine's emerald dragonfly larvae was not significantly altered. There you have it. In order to help the prey, keep one of its predators around!

Don't Pick the Berries

And where do populations of crayfish come from? Well, mature crayfish mate in winter. Once fertilized, the female applies a layer of glue to her underside and then curls her abdomen forward and deposits the eggs in the glue. The female carrying eggs is said to be "in berry" as her eggs resemble tiny, spherical black berries.

Within a month or so, the eggs hatch. The young, that remain attached to their mother, look like miniature adult crayfish.

Should you encounter a crayfish with scores of tiny young clinging to its undercarriage, it is quite a sight. In fact, this sight greeted three of Stillman's regular volunteers.

Late in March, three of the nature center's volunteers saw a female crayfish, loaded with young, heading down one of Stillman's trails. Odds are, she had a burrow nearby. Not surprisingly, these volunteers said I should write about crayfish!

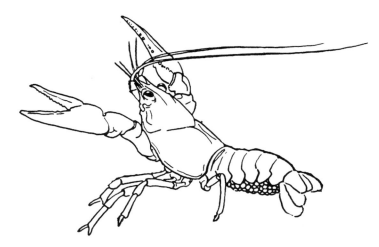

Farewell to a Crustacean, so to speak

To give credit where credit is due, I heavily borrowed from Doug Elliot's wonderful CD titled *Crawdads, Doodlebugs & Greasy Greens* for the story of the Acadians and their lobsters.

But Doug left out one detail. With a little crawdad watching, a Cajun's first attempt to build a chimney ended in disaster. It collapsed and flattened the Acadian right by his log cabin. Of course, you know what was left? A crayfish and a *crushed-cajun.*

Crawdad is my favorite song, honey
Crawdad is my favorite song, babe
Crawdad is my favorite song
Think I've been here way too long
Honey oh babe of mine.

SINISTRAL SNAILS

"Will you walk a little faster?" said a whiting [fish] to a snail,
"There's a porpoise close behind us, and he's treading on my tail."
The further off from England the nearer is to France—
Then turn not pale, beloved snail, but come and join the dance.

—Alice's Adventures in Wonderland
[The Lobster-Quadrille, st. 1 & 3]

While watching my college class work through a lab exercise, I was glancing at a key of aquatic macroinvertebrates. That's a mouthful isn't it?

Aquatic, of course, means that they live in water. Macro means large, but not huge. It really means you don't need a microscope to see them.

The "them" are invertebrates. Invertebrates have skeletons on the outside unlike vertebrates, like us, that have skeletons on the inside. I jokingly tell my students that when you step on a bug (an invertebrate), it goes crunch-squish. When you step on a vertebrate, it goes squish-crunch.

However, there are some invertebrates that wouldn't go crunch-squish. With names like long-solid, spike, and pink heelsplitter, some of the mollusks can be tough customers.

The ones mentioned above are mussels native to the Midwest. Besides mussels, the Phylum Mollusca includes limpets, clams, and snails which brings me back to the invertebrate key.

You see, we often catch aquatic invertebrates here at Stillman when school classes come to do pond study. Animated critters such as crayfish and dragonfly larvae attract most of the attention. Although, the tiny (less than an inch long) clams and snails the students find do hold a certain appeal.

Left Turn Lane

I was in the mollusk section of the key back in the college lab when I was given the following choice: shell sinistral or shell dextral. No, this is not a choice between evil and coordinated shells, rather it is a choice between left-handed and right-handed shells. This begs the question: how can organisms that only have one muscular foot (used for locomotion) be either left-handed or right-handed?

O.K., take a look at the illustrations. If you hold the snail from the top, at its point, and see the opening facing you on the left; you are holding a sinistral snail. If the opening is on the right, you've found a dextral snail.

I have a confession to make. I never noticed the difference until glancing through the key. Now, I regularly check the twist of the snails we catch at the nature center. Why?

These snails are indicators of water quality. Both types of snails are somewhat tolerant of pollution. However, as the degree of pollution increases, you'll be left with left-handed snails.

No, one type of opening doesn't collect more pollutants than the other. It turns out that right-handed snails use an internal gill to transfer dissolved oxygen out of the water. Since polluted water has lower amounts of dissolved oxygen, gilled snails will have a difficult time surviving.

Left-handed snails use a breathing cavity that is similar to a lung. Not surprisingly, these snails come to the surface to periodically fill this cavity. The thin tissue that lines the cavity filters out the oxygen and delivers it to the snail. (Remember, 78% of our air is made up of nitrogen.) Obviously, lunged snails are better equipped to survive in oxygen-poor waters.

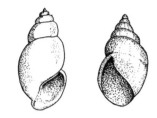

Sex and the Single Snail

There are other interesting differences between these two categories of snails. Most lunged snails are hermaphroditic while most gilled snails have separate sexes.

While self-fertilization is possible for hermaphroditic snails, they generally mate with another individual. As zoologist and author Robert A. Wallace wrote, "As a group, snails have the most bizarre sex lives of any animal." I think we'll just leave it at that.

Well, I was going to leave it at that until a former colleague, who was reading this essay, politely demanded I go into more detail. So, let's continue with the hermaphroditic snails for a bit.

In an aquarium, for example, when one snail catches up or overtakes another, it will be the male. He slithers over the female and covers her extended soft parts with his fleshy foot.

The penis is located behind the right eye stalk. Most times, it is just a small whitish spot under the skin. Now that he's excited, the somewhat flattened appendage emerges. It is big, as long as the snail itself.

Inserting tab A into slot B, as shy folks say, isn't always particularly passionate. While he's getting busy, she sometimes continues to feed, seemingly ignoring him. Meanwhile, he sometimes misses the vagina. Perhaps, he needs more practice. After all, next time he may be a she or s/he.

Both, you ask? Yes, picture this. A male crawls up on a female as described above but then another male slides over the second snail which is now a female for this third snail. Then, another snail crawls on the third snail. There can be as many as fourteen snails in this bumper-to-bumper sexual motorcade. The first one being a female, the last one a male, and all the others are both genders. But, I digress.

Both left and right-handed snails lay their eggs in the spring. The number of eggs ranges from a few to hundreds. Lunged snails lay more eggs than gilled snails. The eggs resemble a small glob of clear mucous with dots inside. We often find these clinging to sticks or leaves during our pond study classes.

Tough Going

When the going gets tough, that is, when a shallow pond either dries up or freezes to the bottom, the pollution-tolerant lunged snails are able to hibernate in the mud. Their life cycle is generally through in a year or less while most gilled snails live from two to five years.

Given the number of things that eat them, it is surprising that snails live as long as they do. A partial list of their predators includes fish, reptiles, waterfowl, and amphibians as well as other invertebrates such as crayfish, leeches, water beetle larvae, and dragonfly larvae.

Snails, as those of you who have had an aquarium know, feed on algae plus decaying plant and animal matter.

Now that we've learned about snails, is there anything we can learn from snails? I'll leave that to John Donne who wrote the following doggerel to Sir Henry Wotton.

And seeing the snail, which everywhere doth roam,
Carrying his own house still, still is at home;
Follow— for he is easy paced— this snail,
Be thine own palace, or the world's thy gaol [jail].

ACKNOWLEDGMENTS

As soon as this book is published, I'll remember somebody I forgot to acknowledge. I have made provisions for this inevitability on the next page.

I am deeply indebted to the Board of the Stillman Nature Center. Without their support, I would not have a career. Fortunately, many of the Stillman Board are retired educators. Their wise advice and consul are truly appreciated.

Several of these same people volunteer to help us teach school classes that visit the center. Some of the articles I wrote were inspired by questions or suggestions that come up during these field trips.

Stillman Nature Center also takes care of disabled birds of prey (i.e. ones that have been hit by a car or shot) that would not survive in the wild. We are lucky to have some of the best volunteer "raptor wranglers" in the business. Not only do these folks help with cleaning but they also assist when we do educational demonstrations. Questions that come up during these programs have generated some of the essays in this collection.

Over the years, I have befriended some raptor and museum colleagues who have encouraged my writing efforts. In particular, I'd like to mention Ron Vasile, Linda Breuer, and mentor Andrea Kane.

Thanks to Taylor Rystrom and my sister Abigail for thoroughly proofreading this text. Any errors you find belong to me. Thank you to my brother, "Chip," for regularly sending nature clippings from the Mountain and Eastern time zones. A heartfelt thanks to my siblings for searching out obscure nature books that I asked for as gifts. Some of those books you'll find listed under *Selected Sources*.

Speaking of gifts, I'd like to tip my hat to all the photographers who donated their wonderful images to this book. Generally, their names appear with their photos.

I also must thank Gillian Kohler for contributing her wonderful line drawings and Jessica Rolczynski for her whimsical cartoons.

Kudos to the college students and summer interns who put up with me as either an instructor or boss. This is the book you said I should write.

Last but not least, I come back to Stillman. Without individual memberships, Stillman Nature Center would not exist. Many who join rarely visit the property, but they all do get our newsletter. I'm assuming those who renew their memberships enjoy the articles. If this assumption is incorrect, please don't tell me.

Finally, I need to thank_____
(put your name here)

If s/he had not helped with_____,
(describe what I forgot)

this book would not be possible.

Mirth first,

Mark Spreyer

Mark Spreyer

SELECTED SOURCES

Wildflowers
Coffey, Timothy. 1994. *The History and Folklore of North American Wildflowers.* Houghton Mifflin Co.
Chouinard, C. (Ed.). 1936. *Fieldbook of Illinois Wild Flowers.* Illinois Natural History Survey
　　Manual 1, Urbana, Illinois.
Davis, M. A. 2009. *Invasion Biology.* Oxford University Press Inc., New York.
Durant, Mary. 1976. *Who Named the Daisy? Who Named the Rose?* Congdon & Weed, Inc., New York.
Headstrom,, Richard. 1968. *Nature in Miniature.* Alfred A. Knopf, New York.
Kirt, R.R. 1995. *Prairie Plants of the Midwest: Identification and Ecology.* Stipes Publishing L.L.C.
Krythe, Mayme R. 1966. *All About the Months.* Harper & Row, Publishers, New York.
Niering, W.A. 1979. *The Audubon Society Field Guide to North American Wildflowers.*
　　Alfred A. Knopf, New York.
Nuzzo, Victoria. 1977. *Our Native Plants.* The Capital Times, Madison, Wisconsin.
Sanders, Jack. 2003. *The Secrets of Wildflowers.* The Lyons Press.

Insects
Borror, D. J., D. M. DeLong, and C. A. Triplehorn. 1976. *An Introduction to the Study of Insects.*
　　Holt, Rinehart and Winston.
Gould, Stephen Jay. 1991. *Ever Since Darwin.* Penguin Books.
Grimaldi, David and Michael S. Engel. 2005. *Evolution of the Insects.* Cambridge University Press.
Mead, Kurt. 2003. *Dragonflies of the North Woods.* Kollath-Stensaas Publishing.
Milne, Lorus and Margery. 1980. *The Audubon Society Field Guide to North American Insects and
　　Spiders.* Alfred A. Knopf, New York.
Stokes, Donald W. 1976. *A Guide to Nature in Winter.* Little, Brown and Company.
Stokes, Donald W. 1983. *A Guide to Observing Insect Lives.* Little, Brown and Company.
Wagner David L. 2005. *Caterpllars of Eastern North America.* Princeton University Press.

Trees
Barlow, Connie. 2000. *The Ghosts of Evolution.* Basic Books.
Barnes, B. V. and W.H. Wagner, Jr. 1981. *Michigan Trees.* The University of Michigan Press, Ann Arbor.
Eastman, John. 1992. *The Book of Forest and Thicket.* Stackpole Books.
Harlow, W. H., E.S. Harrar, and F. M. White. 1979. *Textbook of Dendrology.* McGraw-Hill Book Co.
Nearing, Helen and Scott. 1950. *The Maple Sugar Book.* John Day Company.
Peattie, D. C. 1948. *A Natural History of Trees of Eastern and Central North America.* Houghton Mifflin Co.
Phillips, H. W. 2003. *Plants of the Lewis & Clark Expedition.* Mountain Press Publishing Co.
Plotnik, Arthur. 2000. *The Urban Tree Book.* Three Rivers Press, New York.
Sternberg, Guy and Jim Wilson. 1995. *Landscaping With Native Trees.* Chapters Publishing Ltd.
　　Shelburne, Vermont.

Birds
Bird, D.M. 1999. *The Bird Almanac.* Firefly Books, Buffalo, New York.
Carson, Rachel. 1939. *How About Citizenship Papers for the Starlings?* Nature Magazine.
Carson, Rachel. 1962. *Silent Spring.* Houghton Mifflin Co.
Keppie, D. M. and R. M. Whiting, Jr. 1994. American Woodcock (*Scolopax minor*) In The Birds of
　　North America, No. 100. The Birds of North America Inc. Philadelphia.
Leopold, Aldo 1949. *A Sand County Almanac.* Oxford Univ. Press.

Ridgway, Robert. 1889. *The Ornithology of Illinois, Part I.* Illinois Natural History Survey, Springfield, Illinois.

Spreyer, M. 1990. *Backyard Mynahs: Starlings as Pets.* Journal of the Association Of Avian Veterinarians 4: 88-89.

Spreyer, M. F. and E. H. Bucher. 1998. Monk Parakeet (*Myiopsitta monachus) In* The Birds of North America, No. 322. The Birds of North America Inc.

Tacha, T. C., S.A.Nesbitt, and P. A. Vohs. 1992. Sandhill Crane (*Grus canadensis) In* The Birds of North America, No. 31. The Birds of North America Inc.

Raptors

de la Torre, Julio. 1990. *Owls: Their Life and Behavior.* Crown Publishers, New York.

Craighead, J. J. and F. C. Craighead. 1969. *Hawks, Owls and Wildlife.* Dover Publications.

Duncan, James R. 2013. *The Complete Book of North American Owls.* Thunder Bay Press, San Diego, California.

Hamerstrom, Frances. 1983. *Birds of Prey of Wisconsin.* WI DNR & Madison Audubon Society.

Johnsgard, Paul A. 1988. *North American Owls.* Smithsonian Institution.

Johnsgard, Paul A. 1990. *Hawks, Eagles, & Falcons of North America.* Smithsonian Institution.

Krutch, J. W. and P. S. Eriksson (Eds.). 1962. *A Treasury of Birdlore.* Paul S. Eriksson, Inc., New York.

Medlin, Faith. 1967. *Centuries of Owls.* Silvermine Publishers, Norwalk.

Mockler, Mike (compiler). 1982. *Flights of Imagination.* Blandford Press, Dorset, U.K.

Spreyer, M. 1990. *Living on the Edge: Chicago's Endangered Falcons.* Field Museum of Natural History Bulletin 61: 16-21.

Aquatics

Buffler, Rob and Tom Dickson. 1990. *Fishing for Buffalo.* Culpepper Press, Minneapolis.

Cummings, K. S. and C. A. Mayer. 1992. *Field Guide to Freshwater Mussels of the Midwest.* Illinois Natural History Survey, Champaign, Illinois

Ernst, C.H., J.E. Lovich, and R.W. Barbour. 1994. *Turtles of the United States and Canada.* Smithsonian Institution.

Harding, James H. 1997. *Amphibians and Reptiles of the Great Lakes Region.* University of Michigan Press, Ann Arbor.

Kurta, Allen. 1995. *Mammals of the Great Lakes Region.* University of Michigan Press, Ann Arbor.

McCafferty, W. P. 1983. *Aquatic Entomology.* Jones and Bartlett Publishers.

Mills, Enos A, 1913. *In Beaver World.* Houghton Mifflin Co. (1990 reprint edition from University of Nebraska Press.)

Tyning, Thomas F. 1990. *Guide to Amphibians and Reptiles.* Little, Brown and Company.

Voshell, J. Reese. 2002. *A Guide to Common Freshwater Invertebrates of North America.* The McDonald & Woodward Publishing Co.

Wallace, Robert A. 1980. *How They Do It.* Morrow Quill Paperbacks.